Praise for *With and Witho*

Dorothy Foltz-Gray's writing makes you feel as if you are living her life—and loss—along with her. She conveys the unique connectedness of being a twin, the particular pain of being so violently separated, and her journey toward healing with language that's alive with honesty, heartache, even humor.

—Lisa Delaney, VP/Editor-in-Chief, *Spry magazine/Spryliving.com*,
and author of *Secrets of a Former Fat Girl* (Plume, 2008)

Whoever said "a picture is worth a thousand words" clearly never read anything written by Dorothy Foltz-Gray. Line by line, word by exquisite word, Foltz-Gray recreates not just the world in which we live, the world we see and touch, but the worlds we hold within—the worlds we feel. In *With and Without Her*, her tribute to her late twin sister, Deane, she does it again: With her, we laugh. With her, we weep. This is their story—Deane and Dorothy's, and Dorothy's alone; but for anyone who has ever had a sister, a brother, a best friend, this tender and beautifully written memoir is your story, too.

—Abigail Esman, award-winning writer/essayist,
columnist for *Forbes.com*

With and Without Her is a poignant look inside the deepest of twinships, that of the split egg, an identical, and the wrenching grief and disorientation when that other half is ripped away. Foltz-Gray writes with courageous intimacy about her sister's murder and her own struggle to live on as a singleton.

—Janine Latus, author of the best seller *If I Am Missing
or Dead: A Sister's Story of Love, Murder and Liberation*
(Simon & Schuster, Century/Arrow Books, 2007)

Identical twins—to crib a bit from F. Scott Fitzgerald—". . . are different from you and me." In pulling back the curtain on the uncommonly strong ties that bind siblings who come from a single egg, Dorothy Foltz-Gray chronicles her lifelong journey to find her own self in relation to her twin and soulmate, feeling her way through sameness and separateness until the ultimate separation—her sister's brutal murder—is forced upon her. As Foltz-Gray staggers through the shattered kaleidoscope of grief and pain that follows her sister's death, she creates beauty from horror, excavates self-knowledge from doubt and uncertainty and ultimately finds her own separate, if still uneasy, peace. *With and Without Her* is a poetic tale of connection and separation, confusion and identity that continues to tug at your heart and mind long after you've read the closing lines.

—Norine Dworkin-McDaniel, creator of the family
life blog *Don't Put Lizards In Your Ears*

ALSO BY DOROTHY FOLTZ-GRAY

*Clean Sweep: The Principles of an American Entrepreneur
and the Company He Founded*

Make Pain Disappear

Food Cures (co-author)

*The Arthritis Foundation's Guide to Good Living
with Rheumatoid Arthritis* (editor)

The Arthritis Foundation's Guide to Good Living with Fibromyalgia

Alternative Treatments for Arthritis: An A to Z Guide

Good Living with Osteoarthritis (editor)

WITH AND WITHOUT HER

A Memoir of Being and Losing a Twin

BY DOROTHY FOLTZ-GRAY

Cover photo by Robert Kaster
Visit "Books" on Dorothy Foltz-Gray's website:
www.dorothyfoltzgray.com

Print ISBN 978-0-7867-5420-5

Distributed by
Argo Navis Author Services
www.argonavisdigital.com

For D and D

Preface

I am sitting in a doctor's waiting room, leaning over papers I have brought with me. An employee passes several times and finally stops.

"Are you_____?" she asks me. She names a person I've never heard of.

"No."

"Well, you have a twin." She passes in front of me doing her work. "They say everyone has a twin, and you surely do. You have a twin."

I feel the heat in my face.

"I am a twin," I say. "I had a twin sister who died."

The woman looks at me closely, her banter sobered. "Oh. I'm sorry." She moves on, stops, and smiles. "Then you really are a twin."

People ask me, "Who is your sister?" When she died, my memories of her, of us, became a vault of videotapes in my head, tapes I could play over and over. The first tapes I played were of her murder, what I didn't see, what I imagined. These films had variations, clips I was in, clips of Deane's head turning to the side, clips of her horrible surprise. In my dreams, her office was huge—the lair of a Hollywood mogul where my sister sat behind a huge desk in a leather chair. It was the office of a movie psychologist, elegant, expansive. In reality the office had barely room enough for Deane, her desk, and a patient. When James Palmer appeared, he was less than three feet away from my sister. With a gun, he would have looked enormous, the haunt in her doorway.

Now the memories are muted. It is hard to root for them, like searching an attic without a flashlight. In part, this is because I am practiced at keeping Deane elsewhere, at removing what can't carry me forward. But when I want to, I can include Deane in any setting. She is sitting across from me now, drinking coffee. She wants me to finish my work so we can go into Charleston. She's glad for me that I am writing this book but only if I am glad. It embarrasses her that I reveal so much and talk so long. *How do you do it?* she asks. *Could I do it?* She's proud of me, how I've built my life back. And sad for me, the one unbelievable part of the world.

When I finish my writing session, Deane and I take a long walk and then sit on the beach. With her, I feel quiet, as if I were alone. We look out at the waves and hold hands. This is as close as I get. In a minute she will slip away. Where, after all, can I go with this? I wish she were here. I wish she too were sixty-three. I wish she could tell me everything.

I have now lived as long without her as with her. Why have I gone back to fetch her once more? For two decades I practiced only the future, certain that if I looked back, I would not return to anything like a healthy present. Like a girl in a fairy tale full of superstition, I spun the next day and the day after, threads to another life where Deane would not be all I thought about. But thirteen years ago, an agent suggested that I write a book about Deane, about being and losing a twin. And as soon as she suggested it, I knew it was time to look back, to sort through what it meant to be a twin, to find out if I was still a twin or someone who could only remember what it meant to be a twin. I wanted to find out; I was ready to find out what had happened to Deane at her office that day, details I could not ask about then. I owed Deane the courage to look at what she had faced. And I wanted to do what writers do: make sense out of what cannot be explained. By looking at Palmer, his boyhood, his wife, and family, I could feel sorrow for a boy whose own life did not track the way he'd hoped. By moving into Deane's life and death, I know her/myself once more. No one can take her, not Palmer or death or an untethered earth in this world's sky. Maybe I can't make sense of it all, but while I try, I have Deane back, and I am safe enough.

Chapter 1

I am a twin. My twin sister is dead.

The beginning went like this: we made it up. We sat fused, we said, in our mother's womb. We sat, shuffling cards. We sat, fighting over who would exit first. We bent each other's fingers and kneed each other's spines. We spoke another language. We gave each other nicknames—Ciscus and Karus—two words from our other world. Two words that end in *us*.

We were each other's mother. More than our mother. We swam to each other in our watery world and clung, waiting to be born, arguing over who would lead. I won. First into the world. Eight minutes later, my sister arrived. My father in his suit and tie vaulted through the hall of the Catholic hospital.

"I want to see the doctor," he said, dismissing the nurse who told him he had two babies. He held us, four pounds each, in the palms of his hands, bending over the bed where my mother lay.

"Name them Tomasina and Tomasona," our Uncle Tommy, my father's brother, suggested—the first of a lifetime of jokes about the bafflement we posed. *Give them two names almost indistinguishable. Like they are. Two people. One face.* But I never believed we were identical. Her face was round and soft and open; mine was longer and sharper. And far more than features made her distinct, although I am practiced now in keeping her vividness faint. Next to her, I was querulous, impulsive. She was quiet and observant, sensual and thoughtful.

Our mother never thought we were identical either. She loved us to the eclipse of our brother, Jeff, older by four and a half years. He became, not intentionally, a shadow. In early pictures, he is standing behind us, Deane and me in white baby chairs, their backs shaped like oyster shells. Our mother sits beside us in starched, full skirts. She talks of two babies as constant work, feeding one and then the other, dressing one and next the other. And starting over. But the pictures show something else—her full, red lips, her unruffled happiness. In silent home movies, she is always bending over us. Or we are rushing toward her, our lips shaping "Mama." We move in and out of an oscillating spray of water, running away from its mouth and toward it. We are naked except for diapers, our shoulder blades pointing backward like wings, our ribs like steps to our necks. We seem the blur of one image, a tape of one moment played over and over. And then we stop and throw our arms around each other, a spasm of spiny thinness.

My mother could keep the stories about us straight. I was the one who always said no; Deane, yes. I stuck my tongue out at strangers. Deane smiled. But my early memories are rarely of two people. I am Deane, and I am myself. What happened to whom? Did I cut myself with the razor? Did Deane smear cold cream over my mother's green satin dress? Was it I who crawled into the corner away from the fierce dog who wanted to eat me?

A twin does not own memories like other people do. Detaching my acts from Deane's was like pulling gum from a shoe: the threads stretch out in all directions but they can't exactly separate. We didn't mind, because it was useless to mind. We were one entity Deanedorothy. Besides, we could tell our stories either way. If I was telling one, any part could be mine, and that was true for Deane as well. Except for the stories Mom kept straight. My tongue out. Deane's tears. Deane's bottom on the hot grid of a floor furnace. My pulling the boy's hair.

No, Deane pulled the boy's hair. For that, a herd of grown-ups set her in the corner. But I felt I had done it. Deane's punishment, my misery. And this is any twin's secret: our cells float separately in the world. They separate and float in two bodies. But the first encoding stays. Everyone thinks this is happening to Deane. But it is happening to me.

The question people always asked us: "Can you tell yourselves apart?" Deane and I knew what people wanted to hear: "No, we can't. Don't worry. We are as confused as you are." So we told them the story of the mirrors. One summer our good-sport parents took us and friends to an amusement park that had a house of mirrors. In we went. Like everyone else, Deane and I lost each other among the reflections. But unlike the others, we bashed into the mirrors, thinking we had found each other. People loved that story because it confirmed what they perceived: a likeness so profound it could confuse anyone, even us.

Now I am a singleton, but I remain a twin. Or I should say, I have had two lives, one with Deane and one without her.

Chapter 2

The story of my sister's death is hard to tell because it is so horrible. If I mention that I am a twin, listeners grin and begin to ask questions.

"Are you identical?"

"We were. She died."

"At birth?"

"No, when she was thirty-two."

Now the speaker is alarmed. "Was she sick?"

And when I answer, I will lose Deane again because my listener will not want to talk about her.

On Thursday evening, August 13, 1981, Deane and I talk on the phone about last-minute details: the next day, she is flying to Knoxville, Tennessee, to spend ten days with me. We are going to celebrate: That same morning she is handing her doctoral thesis in psychology to a typist, finished at last. But she is grumpy, exhausted.

"I'm not ready. I'm not packed. I'm fat." I can hear her cat purring on her chest where she rests the receiver.

"You are ready. You don't need anything. You're not fat." My exasperation shows. I am tired of this conversation.

"You don't think so? I have to get up at six tomorrow to get my thesis to the typist."

"A good thing," I remind her testily. "What you've been waiting for."

"It doesn't feel like it. I don't feel like it."

"Okay." I'm done. I'm pacing my kitchen, pouring a glass of wine. She knows it. We hang up, out of sorts. In a few minutes she calls back.

"I didn't want to end that way."

"You'll feel better tomorrow. We'll celebrate."

"Okay," she says, brighter. "Okay."

I wake at eight and go downstairs to set a bottle of champagne in the refrigerator. I wrap a belt I'd bought for her, the card addressed to "Dr. Deane." I sit down at my desk to write. I am writing poetry about the roofers who hammer into the night on my neighbor's roof, about the way they sit, their knees up like repeating roofs, how they yell at each other across the shingles, *Hey boy, you quitting?*

Weeks before, the Tennessee Arts Commission awarded me an individual artist's grant of $5,000 for my poetry—in those days, enough for me to live the year on, or close, if I was careful. I was elated with the nod. I had asked a poet I had met only once—Charles Wright of Virginia—to recommend me because he had given a long poem of mine first place in another contest. He did recommend me, noting with humor how odd it was to recommend someone he hardly knew. But he did it with grace and humor, and his recommendation clearly had some weight.

So I write today because now, with this grant, it is my job. The state has said so.

But I am also impatient and hardly able to concentrate. In eight hours, she will be here.

In Cambridge, Massachusetts, Deane packs her bags. She puts in two t-strap T-shirts for me, and a box of our favorite almond pastries. She gets in her blue Volkswagen Rabbit and drives to the typist. She climbs back in her car for the drive to Stoney Brook Counseling Center in Chelmsford, where she works as a psychologist. She walks in and teases the receptionist about eating at her desk. "Oh, doughnuts today, eh, Lorraine," she says, laughing a little bit. She pours herself a cup of coffee and walks down the hall to her office for her ten o'clock appointment.

Outside, in the center's parking lot, James Palmer sits in a blue Datsun sedan. He has brown hair and eyes, a mustache, a handsome, soft face. He is twenty-seven and wants to be a policeman, like his father before him. The winter before, he had been meeting with two doctors at the center: a psychiatrist named Alan Shields and my sister. Palmer told Deane he had a terrible secret: *I dress in women's clothes.*

Is it so terrible?

The next week he did not show up for his appointment—or the next—although in June, he saw Dr. Shields once more. Deane was glad not to see him. He scared her. She told me this as we drove along Storrow Drive when I visited her in February. She sometimes told me stories of her patients without using names, telling me what moved her, what scared her, what made her feel lucky.

"One woman," she says, "every time I see her, she says, 'Just give me a cup of poison, doctor. Just give me a cup of poison.'"

"What do you say?"

"'I can't give you that, but how about a cup of tea? I can get you that.'"

"Do they scare you?" I ask.

"One did. But he's not been back," she says. "He told me he was a transvestite. And he just scared me. It was so hard the way he told me. So painful—as if he couldn't stand to tell me, and he couldn't stand not to." She looks at me, gripping the blue Volkswagen steering wheel with her gloved hands. "Some patients just make you feel scared—maybe the way they feel. He wants to be a policeman. I'm glad he hasn't come back." We drive into Cambridge and pull into the garage underneath a little bistro where we'll eat lunch. "Let's eat," Deane says, and that's the last she talks about her patients.

That wintry morning in February, Palmer was no more than a tale she told to bring her life into my sight. He was only a story, not yet *the* story.

At 10 a.m., Palmer gets out of his car and walks to the door of the wood-shingled counseling center, located in the center of a small suburban strip mall. He walks in, looks into the waiting room, turns around as if he is going out, and spins back again. In his navy pinstripe suit jacket he marches past Lorraine, the twenty-three-year-old receptionist who's talking on the phone at her desk, who figures Palmer knows what he's doing; and he marches past Nancy, the office manager also on the phone, who assumes he's going to the rest room. He walks to Alan

Shields's office and opens the door. Shields, tall and thin with a long face, big, square glasses, and a head of black, curly hair, is standing, talking to social worker Barbara Kaplan, Deane's friend, newly married. Kaplan, a small woman with a warm smile, who does not usually go to the office on Fridays, is meeting with a consultant instead. But the consultant is unexpectedly out of town, so Kaplan has arranged to see a client from nine to ten. Afterward, she goes to Shields's office to chat. When the door opens, Kaplan turns and sees Palmer—a stranger to her—standing in the doorway, holding a gun. What kind of joke is this? she thinks. Palmer lifts a .357 Magnum handgun and shoots Shields once, hitting him in the cheek; a bullet that goes through his skull and out the back of his head. Kaplan begins to scream. Palmer shoots her in the eye. As she ducks, she covers her head with her hands. A second bullet slices off the tip of her right ring finger.

Deane and her client Donna hear the shots. Donna has just handed Deane a picture of her little girl. Deane rises from her chair, the baby picture in her hand, and Palmer opens the door to her office. Deane turns her head, "Oh no." Squared, he shoots her once in the head, and she falls chest down, her face turned to the side, and he shoots her in the neck. A bullet ricochets off a wall, grazing Donna on the ankle. She raises her arms, pulls her legs up. "Please don't hurt me." He steps back outside the room, and Donna counts the shots she'd heard: six shots, and he can't come back.

Nancy hears what sounds like a cap gun. Bang, bang. Bang, bang. And again, bang, bang. She puts her call on hold. Lorraine, next to her, falls to a crouch underneath her desk, shaking. Nancy joins her, holding the telephone, her fingers dialing the police. Three patients—a nineteen-year-old girl, Sondra; a six-year-old girl, Jennifer; and Iris, her mother, thirty—hide under chairs in the waiting room.

Palmer goes back to Deane's office with a second gun in his hand, looking at her, dropping the gun to the floor.

"Please don't shoot me," Donna says again.

"Get out of here," Palmer answers. "Hurry up," he says, backing out of Deane's office.

Donna runs past him, past Shields's body, his long legs in the hallway—

the hall and the waiting room now empty. She pulls on the knob of the outside door. *He's locked us in*, she thinks.

Yet the door opens and she runs outside, past the first office and the next, turning to see if Palmer is following her.

He marches down the hall behind her, just as he had entered, the bell jingling on the door as he leaves.

After Palmer runs out, the mother pulls her daughter from under the chair, pushes her into an empty office. The other patient and the two office workers lock the door to the central area and go into an office where Nancy calls the police again, then she ventures down the hall. She sees Shields lying on the floor and Barbara Kaplan sitting in a chair, her face in her hands. And she sees Deane, also on the floor, her head and neck covered with blood. The sound Nancy makes fills the hallway, her voice a siren. She runs back to the front and calls an ambulance twice. When the mother hears the police cruiser arrive, she opens the window and screams for help.

Lorraine shifts the phones to an answering service. Donna has run to a medical office several doors down, bursting in on pediatrician Irving Newman and his patient. *There's been a shooting.*

Officer John Bell, the first officer to get a call, arrives in the parking lot at 10:11, not a person in sight. He draws his .38 revolver, runs to the clinic door, opens it, calling, "Police. Where is he?"

"I don't know," someone answers, "I think he left."

Bell runs down the hall, sees the bodies and the abandoned gun, and radios for three ambulances and for more help. Two more officers arrive, one from the police station, one from the streets. Officer Mark Burlamachi kneels beside Shields, finds no pulse, and heads to Deane's office, where she lies unconscious, holding a picture of her patient's baby, her head toward the door, a gun a foot away, the barrel pointed toward her back. He finds a pulse. He guesses Deane is a nurse. Another policeman arrives: Sergeant Leslie Adams, who has known Palmer, or Jim, for twenty-seven years. *Jimmy*, he calls him. They turn Deane onto her back. Then the pediatrician Newman, balding with a graying goatee, arrives and takes over. Deane's body is in shock, her pulse weak. He gives her oxygen and something to stabilize her blood pressure, her pulse; he keeps her alive. His nurse arrives and gives her CPR.

Another doctor, Bill Beaucher, arrives from Newman's medical office and tends to Kaplan's bullet wound below her eye, in a room near the one where Shields lies dead. Later, Newman says he is proud of how they worked, like emergency-room doctors without equipment.

A newspaper photo shows paramedics loading Deane onto an ambulance, her head to the side, her curly hair, her closed eyes, her right foot without a shoe. How calm her face looks. This terror now past her, somewhere else, streaming up. I want to put her shoe on.

Chapter 3

At 11:40 a.m., when I answer the phone, Deane's roommate Pat, a phlegmatic woman with sharp, straight hair and a spare manner, is on the line.

"Something bad has happened."

I imagine Deane in a car accident.

"Deane's been shot."

I see her arm shot.

"She's in critical condition." (Critical condition, I later learn, is the way the news or a hospital says *death*.) "At St. Joseph's Hospital."

I get off the phone, and I begin to scream. I run to the bottom of the stairs, and I scream for my husband. Dan, too, is a writer—and a teacher at a community college—free to write at home in the summers. He calls the hospital. They confirm that Deane is critical. They will call back, they say. I lie down on the kitchen floor as if it is safer there, somehow, below the news, a place that might swallow me, my terror.

Once, four years before, when Deane and I both lived with our husbands in Ann Arbor, Michigan, I was walking home from work, a route that took me past Deane's house. I decided to stop. The doors were open, and I called out. No answer. I called again. Where was she, with the doors wide open? And then I saw her climbing the outdoor basement steps with the laundry. "Oh, Deane, I was so scared something had happened to you." She poured us sodas and set out cheese and crackers, and we sat for a while in her living room. What is too frightening to think, we do think: that we could lose each other, that one of us could die, will die, before the other.

Now, that August day years later, I call my mother, who also begins to scream. She hangs up to call my father at his law office. I call Sarah, Deane's best friend, who hangs up to make calls. I lie on the bed watching nothing, the phone dumb.

Sarah, who lost her own brother years before, calls back and tells me in a low, steady voice to come to Boston and to pack a lot of clothes. A kindergarten teacher, she understands the value of clear direction.

"Where was she shot?" I ask.

"In the head."

"Can they operate?"

"No."

That evening, Deane's other roommate Lynn, dark and zaftig, rides home from work on a bus. Deane knew she and Lynn would become friends when, one evening, Lynn pulled a tablecloth off its table and threw it around her shoulders to wear for the evening. Now Lynn reads the newspaper's headlines over another passenger's shoulder: *Shootings in Chelmsford*. She wonders if Deane knows about them. She will ask her when she gets home.

At the hospital, Kaplan's new husband sits outside the operating room where doctors work to save Barbara's eye. The next day she asks about Deane, but no one wants to answer.

I hang up the phone and pack my clothes, but I pack thoughtlessly. Dan makes plane reservations, and by mid-afternoon we leave the house to drive to the airport, remembering as we leave that we have no front door to lock, that we are having the front door refinished. We remove an inside door from its hinges, prop it where the front door should be, and get in the car. As we leave, I look out the window at the fuchsia crepe myrtles blooming in our yard, their vivid August life.

For the next eight hours, I sit through two plane rides, Knoxville to Pittsburgh, Pittsburgh to Boston. At the Pittsburgh airport, I edge toward the window where no one will try to talk to me, try to make me normal. I pick up magazines and turn the pages without reading. I cannot read or speak or cry. (In movies, when the bereaved cry as soon as they are told of death, I now know the movie director has not had the dry, numb call.) We land in Boston close to midnight, the airport empty except for artificial light. A friend of Deane's and his wife wait at the entrance of the terminal to pick us up. Their faces are frightened, even embarrassed. I ask the man if Deane is still alive. *There are no brain waves.* I hear the words, but I refuse them. This is not the person who will tell me my sister is dying.

I am hurtling toward my parents. When I see them, I will feel safe to hear what I now cannot. I think about my mother's scream, its quaver when I said Deane had been shot. They will have arrived from Philadelphia hours before, and we have not spoken since late morning.

My father will have gone quiet, thinking through the practical, the details: the air tickets, the hotel, the rental car—details he is grateful for. They tell him how to guide my mother on this wordless path to my sister.

My mother will be numb—the world, as she has always known, a menace. Her baby brother died when she was three, and her alcoholic father sometimes disappeared for days, leaving her with a depressed and angry mother, whose scoldings were worse than a slap on the leg. My father's joke about my mother: *She would have you drive in armored tanks if she could.* And now she knows she was right: the world has not felt safe, because it isn't.

Chapter 4

I am born first, eight minutes ahead of Deane, eight minutes that we talk about throughout our lives. Why did Deane loiter? We make up answers: I'd pushed her aside, blocking her way. We fought. "I'm going." "No, I am," Deane says, grabbing my index fingers and twisting them to the side—bends I carry into the world. She screams at my stubborn selfishness, my need for control. She is on the agenda, ready to get with it. And then once I am gone, well, what a relief. A few minutes of peace, a swim in freer quarters. She hangs out in the pod. She watches how things go for me. We imagine our birth as collaboration, a joint affair, the echo of our personalities.

Our mother doesn't know she is having twins, although she might have guessed, her stomach so round our father threatened to roll her with a hoop stick. Still, it's her stomach, not us, that grows big. We are born a month early, January 23, 1949, in a Catholic hospital in Fort Smith, Arkansas, where my mother's parents live, where she has gone to stay while our father starts his FBI job in Little Rock.

My parents met years before, when my mother was fourteen, my dad nineteen. His father, a Fort Smith doctor, had lost money in the Depression. "The one with the lowest grades has to stay out of college a year," he told his four college-age children. So, for a year, my dad left Washington and Lee to work as a bellboy in a Fort Smith hotel. One day my mom walked in on her father's arm. "That's a mighty pretty daughter you have, Mr. Mitchell," my father said. And she was—a tall, thin mix of Bette Davis and Lucille Ball, with huge round eyes set far apart, thick, red curly hair, and a full mouth made for a lipstick ad. Soon after, Dad asked her out on a double date. He and the other two people had read *Gone with the Wind,* and my mother thought they were all stuck up. And Dad seemed so old with his slicked-black hair, his receding hairline, his boxer build.

The Foltzes knew the Mitchells in that small Southern town, and Dad shrugged off her high school shyness. Four years later, when Mom went to Monticello College in Arkansas, Dad invited her to Washington and Lee in Virginia, still there in law school. Each weekend he thought he'd won her, but after every visit, she turned cool.

"What's the matter, Mitch?" he asked her on weekday phone calls.

"Nothing," she answered and let the mute air speak for her.

Decades later, as she was dying, my father told me he loved the challenge she offered, her elusiveness. By the time she graduated from the University of Arkansas at age twenty-one, the war had started, my father was stationed in San Francisco with the FBI, and Pearl Harbor was only months away.

"You'd better marry him, Deane," her bossy mother (my grandmother) said. "He won't wait for you." For my mother, the pair and their pressure were formidable. It's not that she didn't like my father. But she was young and pretty, and when he wasn't around, she still had suitors and freedom. She knew she had to marry—her friends all were—but she was terrified of sex—what all young men thought about, and nothing a well-brought-up woman should want. Still, she hated her mother's disapproval, and she was afraid she'd lose her chances, the good men gone to war. It was easier to let her mother push her to yes. A relief really. They married in the chapel of Grace Cathedral in San Francisco on my father's birthday, December 31, 1941, almost a month after Pearl Harbor. From the start, he was my grandmother's stern replacement. Within months, he bought his bride a back brace to improve her posture.

She greets him at the apartment door, puzzled by the apparatus he carries.

"It'll be good for your back, Deanie," he says, handing her the brace. "It'll help your posture."

She doesn't look at him, taking the brace and putting it in the hall closet. In pictures with San Francisco spread out below her, she looks tentative, reserved, her shoulders still rolled forward. In 1944, their first child, Jeff, is born.

Now my mother looks happier, her arms around her tow-headed boy. He is the love of her life. To him, she is perfection, a thought no one has ever had for her before. Together they spend hours laughing while they read *Winnie the Pooh* or rolling Jeff's wagon up and down the street while he hunts for Indians.

When Mom tells him a baby is coming, our prescient brother, in love with Babar the elephant, asks for twin elephants. But we are just a little over four pounds each, stuck in incubators. Our father stares through the hospital windows where we lie in adjacent incubators, jaundiced and tiny. He turns and walks down the corridor, buying a pack of cigarettes, a habit he had quit. But he resumes under the pressure of triple patriarchy and sits in the fathers' waiting room, shaking his head, telling anyone who will listen that he has twin girls.

In a few hours, he enters our mother's hospital room, where she sits propped, cradling us. "I have no idea what to name them, Ed," says our mother, reaching for her icy Coca-Cola as she hands him two babies. Our strong father, who tracks down spies threatening the Free World, takes one of us in each palm, bending over the soft mattress, afraid he will drop us.

For days after our birth, we are A and B. Later Deane and I convince ourselves that we were mixed, a common fantasy among identical twins: she is really A, and I am B. This means that I am Deane and she is Dorothy. We believe this and ponder it like a menu of options. It is easy to believe. Our identities from the outset seem arbitrary, interchange-able. Identity is a kind of faith, like the belief in a round earth or a sky that cannot fall. The mutability of the basic doesn't bother us. I might as well be Deane, and she me. The whole world tells us it doesn't matter. It tells us because it doesn't know who we are, because it doesn't know our names, because we are repeating patterns like printed wallpaper or paper cutouts. The content of a name, the world tells us, is nothing. For us, a name doesn't matter. What I feel is what Deane feels. Who I am is what-ever Deane is. When we play this game of reversal, it is a short one.

When I believe I am truly Deane, I am the same. The game runs dry. It's much more fun to pretend I am a horse.

On our tiny wrists pink alphabet blocks read *Baby A Foltz, Baby B Foltz*. We remain unnamed, and our mother is exhausted. She lies back on the hospital bed and puts on lipstick, smoothing it into her mouth's corners with the tip of her little finger, perpetually stained. The nurse carries us in one at a time, one for each breast. But milk is scant, and my mother's nipples hurt. After the first day, she is crying, "What will we name them? How will I nurse two babies?" The nurses don't know either. We peck at our mother's chest like baby birds, and our cries sound like birds too. We are so tiny, we lie like shadows in the fold of each elbow.

The nurses try formula. One night we swallow three ounces and throw it all back up, one after the other like staggered fountains. Our papery veins collapse from dehydration, and we suck on dry air. All night the nurses ask our thirst to win over our spastic stomachs. An ounce is a victory that moves fear down the hall.

Our grandmother Dottie is critical of our mother's indecisiveness. "You have to do something, Deane. You can't just call them A and B." Our grandmother is a big woman with breasts that could feed six babies. Her lips thin as a pin, she bends over our mother, our mother named Dorothy Deane Mitchell Foltz. "Why don't you name one Dorothy and the second one Deane?" This is such a relief our mother does not hear it as a question, but a command. The bracelets come off, replaced with new long names: Dorothy Jane, Florence Deane. We are D and D, a formula of ease, of correctness. When the teacher doesn't know who we are, it's *Hello, D and D.* When the choirmaster isn't sure, it's *Take your places, D and D.* Later we are happy for the *Jane* and the *Florence*, the foreign objects that make us different. There is nothing alike about those two names, not even the way our lips move when we say them—like a suburb of distinction away from identical row houses and block streets. Later I read about a survey of twin names: four sets out of ten have names that begin with the same initial or are linked in some way; the figure rises to 50 percent for girl twins.

After ten days, doctors allow us to go home. Dottie stands waiting at the hospital door, formidable and padded in her winter coat. It is cold, but our mother's coat won't button, so our father settles her into the car, wrapping a blanket around her middle while the nurses wait, holding us like white packages from the butcher. We ride to Dottie's tiny brick house, where our brother waits for twin elephants. When we walk in, Grandfather Harry has Jeff on his knee, eating sugared orange slices. Jeff runs to our mother and flings himself at her knees. "Where are the elephants?" He unfolds the blankets that cover our faces, fascinated and repulsed. "What are these?" In pictures he is no longer smiling.

Chapter 5

It is past twelve, a starless night when we reach St. Joseph's Hospital. A black cross rises from the roof cornice, and from inside, the dimmed lights of night duty add a blue cast to the windows. We are bending the rules, violating the regular rounds of the hospital.

An attendant in reception directs us to the floor where my parents wait. Deane's friends who have driven us remain behind. The elevator doors open, and I see my parents leaning against the wall opposite the elevator, their leaden faces, and I realize what I already knew: my sister is dying.

My sister's estranged husband, Art, walks toward me. His bearded face is twisted and small: "I always loved her," he says. I know he means it, this tall, thin man I hardly know, though I have known him since he and Deane met seven years before. He is both quiet and reserved, hidden really. During their time together, Deane became quieter too, more muted. For him, I always felt a storm of feelings—anger that he had taken Deane, that she had chosen someone I couldn't know, who changed, and finally hurt her with an affair and perhaps more by his disappearance, even as he remained.

"Where is she?" I ask. "I want to see her."

My father hesitates. But all of us walk down a hall into a small room with a single bed, and there, her head swollen and swathed, her face bruised, her chest inflated by the ventilator that keeps her alive, is no one who resembles my sister. She looks grotesque, inflexible, huge-shouldered, dark, and battered. Beside her, a respirator rises and falls, its end pieces winding into her throat. Her brain has no activity, but the rhythm of her heart repeats on the green monitor next to her bed. I bend close to her, close enough to whisper in her ear. The machine keeps up its pumping. I hold her hand, more like her now than her face, my face. This cannot be Deane. I want to do whatever the doctors did not, cross whatever border biology has set, see if I can wriggle past the barriers until I find her and pull her back.

I look up and see my father first, his face slack with sorrow. He is watching me, but he is silent, his disbelief crashing into mine. My mother too is silent, her head down, her face pale with fear. She cannot look at me, as if she is already far away, too afraid to be fully present. She places her hand on the foot of the bed, not quite on Deane's foot but close enough. My father takes my elbow to pull me back out of the room.

We walk down the hall to another hospital room that the nurses have lent my family—a kind of drawing room to receive friends and flowers. But tonight the room is empty. In fact, the whole floor is dark and silent. It is 1 a.m., and the quiet heightens our sense that we have left the accustomed world. Dan and I sit on the edge of the bed, my mother on a chair, her profile to us.

She has receded, darkened in the fourteen years since Deane and I left home for college. Our raising had been her career, and now her days are spent running errands for our father, playing golf and bridge, or sitting in the tiny TV room we call *The Sardine Lounge*, watching television game shows while she works the daily crossword puzzle. Although she doesn't say, she seems unhappy, bored, uncertain how to keep going in a life that keeps getting smaller. She talks sometimes of volunteering at a nursery school, but she says this only when Deane and I worry over what she is doing. She doesn't want us to think she is lost. "I read," she says uncertainly, when Deane and I question her.

Now she sits watching my father, trying to believe that he will fix this, as he has fixed so many other things. As I watch her, I realize I have seen this quiet in her only once before, when she got the call that her father had had a heart attack. It was the day before Thanksgiving, when Deane and I were in the fourth grade.

She stood in the hallway of our house, her shoulders sloped in her coat as we all prepared to leave. My parents dropped all three of us at friends to stay while they flew to Fort Smith, my mother as afraid of flying in a propeller plane as she was of losing her father. By Thursday, he was dead, and when my mother came back, she sat for a moment on the living room sofa, then fell to one side, her face weeping into the brown cushion, her thin shoulders heaving. She had always felt adored by her round-faced, round-bellied, balding, and white-haired father. But my grandmother in a moment of unconscious cruelty remarked to my mother's sister that she had always been her father's favorite. I imagined my mother's surprise, how hard it must have been to breathe, watching the certainty of her father's love evaporate. Her tears were grief and fury, and I was scared by such a lethal mix, afraid I wouldn't get back my mother as she had been.

She is the same tonight, rooted to the chair, but not yet weeping, She is again the woman in the hallway, slope-shouldered, afraid of what's coming. I begin to realize, as I will many times over the next months, that I can count on her for nothing but her sorrow and the certainty of love—not small, but not useful either. Even my father, who rebels against his shock by searching for information he can act on—brain surgeons, who are they, where are they, what anyone can do, what power it will take for him to make anything happen—even my father cannot face facts the way I have: what we have left is death. My parents—so different in their strengths—are nonetheless the same in this: they give Deane to me, and every decision we make about her is mine.

Eight months before, my father retired from the Campbell Soup Company after twenty-eight years there, first as the director of personnel (his boss thought he was a tough labor negotiator because he'd been in the FBI and negotiated labor contracts at Borg-Warner, an appliance giant in Cleveland), then president of Campbell Soup International, and finally head of corporate affairs. But he could not retire. He had buddies in a downtown law office that invited him to join their practice. In the last months, he'd set up in their satellite office a few miles from home. "Maybe I'll bring in a little business," he said. He was excited to be dusting off his law degree. He was looking forward to bringing business discipline to the practice, he said, appalled that it didn't run like the corporate giant he was used to. He didn't have a secretary either—my mother was her unwilling substitute—and I saw for the first time his helplessness about simple tasks that I now understood his assistant had done for him: paying bills, tracking deadlines, keeping a conveyor belt of paper and appointments moving. Now he was off track.

In this moment, as I see him working through the details of Deane's dying, I realize he has never tackled the implacable. Ketchup runs can be halted, employees can be fired, candy companies can be made over, but death is a concrete floor with no give, although he is looking for it everywhere.

I am shaking and cold. As my parents and I talk, what we say makes no more sense than Deane's swollen head. Our words pool together and hover on the floor between us.

In a while, I walk out of the room, and a nun comes toward me. She takes my hands and looks into my face. Her own face is cupped by her habit, distilling her features, the round, clear eyes, the soft, aging skin. She bends her head toward mine and says what no one else can hear, says what no one else could have said: "Congratulations. Your sister is in paradise." I want to step inside her, to be that certain. I envy her belief. What do I feel at her words except reassurance; here at last is someone who knows something about Deane beyond brainwaves and .357 magnums and death. For months afterward, I assume that Deane can color the sky pink or control the songs on the radio or open up a parking space or turn water to glitter on a fall day. She is everywhere because I know she would not leave me. My certainty makes the world's mysteries thin enough to pass through.

My parents have rented a car and drive us to a small motel nearby where they have booked rooms side by side. Dan carries in their bags, our bags. He pulls the covers back, unzips the suitcases, fills glasses with ice and water. He does, as always, what needs doing, his gift to see such needs before anyone else does. I kiss my parents, and Dan and I go to our room next door. We are not speaking, and he knows better than to enter my silence. It is not his way to address emotion head on; he would rather step back, let me talk if I need to. In his parents' house, excess emotions—anger, grief, pride—were unacknowledged embarrassments, smothered by his mother's laughter, his father's silence. Dan became a tuning fork, sensitive to emotion but trained in receding from it. So he does tonight, absent any cues from me except a tight-lipped silence. We are also too exhausted to speak at 2 a.m., a life away from where we woke.

In a few minutes, we turn on the TV to have noise, distraction. The channel is set to local news, and Deane, her colleagues, her gunman are today's headlines. Is the announcer screaming? Deane's clinic and the ambulance and the voiceover of death cram into our room. *Gunman kills one, injures three at Chelmsford clinic.* The world is full of this news, and the TV forces our immersion. Except the news objectifies the personal, screens it with a lens, these deaths of strangers by a stranger, a story that makes any watcher for one moment feel lucky. A piece of the world goes crazy, but you're not there.

We turn the TV off, click off the lights but do not sleep or touch. At last I go into the bathroom, lie down on the cold tile floor, and begin to cry for the first time that day. Only the sound I make is one I have never heard my body make before. It is the sound I have heard when news reporters cover foreign disasters, photographing women whose heads turn up and mouths hang open, who scream more than cry, and what journalists film is an abstraction called *mourning*. As if a cry could push away what these women know, as if their bodies too are in battle with death. As mine is.

Danny comes to me and guides me to my feet, holding my elbow, his arm around my waist. "Come back to bed," he says, almost a whisper. He doesn't say I need sleep or that tomorrow will be long and hard, but it is what I know he means. I slip under the covers, and Dan turns over, his back to me, as he always sleeps. But for me, sleep cannot subdue the stimulant of shock and disbelief.

So, once again, I get up. I feel more at ease sitting near Dan. I sit in an armchair and write. Like my father, I too need something to do. I can draft Deane out of death or tunnel my way in with words, paving a path to her. I begin that night what I will do for months: hunt for what will bring her back. This black and white on a page: this is my key, and I keep going like a scientist accumulating data on faith until one day the pieces fit and death didn't happen. I write until dawn, and then I get back into bed to sleep for several hours until my sister's face wakes me in a dream, and I hear my parents next door. I get up and put on the same clothes I wore yesterday, clothes that can't protect me from the Boston cold.

I walk next door to my parents' room and knock. "Did you sleep?" I ask, leaning to give my mother a hug. She is dressed but distracted, rushing to finish, to put makeup on her pale face, to get her earrings on. It irritates me that she is dressing as she always does, can even consider makeup and jewelry. I am surprised that this morning her concern for appearance can annoy me. But her reactions are off: she has moved into another world where she will be silent or simply skimming the surface of what she remembers about how to behave. "It's cold," I say. I walk over to my father, who is bending over his suitcase, and kiss him too. He has on a tie, as always, a white shirt, black suit pants. "They have a motel restaurant," he says. "I just spoke to Jeff. He's driving up. He'll be here this afternoon. We should eat something."

Danny and I follow behind them to the restaurant, a clean, clinical place with paper mats and plates of pancakes that rush by on a waitress's arm. We pass a pile of newspapers. "Shooting victim near death" is the headline, and I know I will not eat. We sit down, and I ask for coffee and juice. "You have to eat," my father says. He turns to the waitress. "Add an order of toast."

Chapter 6

Twins sprinkle through our family like coarse salt on an otherwise dark sheet. In the gold filigree frame at the top of my parents' bookcase stands the photo of our great-grandmother and great-aunt, the Love sisters, their joined hands and identical somber faces both mysterious and familiar to Deane and me. We understand in their dittoed faces the eerie improbability we also present to the world. Inside the pleated folds of white dresses, the high collars choking their necks like an extra pair of hands, sits one person and then another. But they look no different than repeating commas on a page. Their mouths straighten in the same way, their parted black hair pulled back, hidden behind the long, white necks. One person has been inked, imprinted on the other side of the page. Except their joined hands tell another story, their fingers entwined until we cannot untwist them, know whose is whose.

Years later, I read a *New Yorker* article that studies a painting by Raymond Han: twin girls in black dresses in front of a green and orange globe of the world turn their bodies toward each other, their unsmiling faces facing out. The hands of their outer arms clasp so that the arms form the lower half of a circle their almost touching heads and sloping shoulders complete. The reviewer talks of disquietude, of a split personality, a double vision. But what I see is necessity: they are inevitably linked. Together their circled arms form the globe they need.

As Deane and I are linked, as the Love sisters are. Seeing them, my sister and I, like anyone else, want to laugh. And why not? Twins are laughable, like Tweedledee and Tweedledum. Other repeats are not: a field of tulips, a row of maples, a factory of cheeses, a wall of bricks. They are miraculous maybe, utilitarian, even beautiful, but not a joke. Except in humans. Because the eye wants to argue. Human duplication is science fiction, a way to say machinery or robots or aliens have taken over. Our brains say, *Not so.*

But my sister and I do not think *we* are funny or even like machines. We laugh at our great-grandmothers and still do not *feel* the joke we reside in. Because for twins, looks are for other people. We are—as other people are—what we feel inside. Only Deane has her face. Not me. I am what I feel about myself and what I feel about Deane. That's what gets mixed up, not our faces.

Our father and his twin, Cissy, are also framed in glass as toddlers in identical white smocks, identical straight bobs. My sister and I lay on the living room floor holding the photograph and stared at them. They looked to us like the little boy in the shoe store, Buster Brown doubled: the same sailor collars, the same chubby faces. And their faces were identical. But we felt sorry for them. Because he is a boy and she is a girl. Their grown-up faces told us what we believed was true. They were not alike. She had tiny feet, like Cinderella, and a small, sharp nose, and lips that curved into an oval. He had a big, long face with round cheeks and a nose twisted by boxing injuries. He called Cissy at Christmas, but otherwise they never speak. Deane and I could not imagine such separation. When our father talked about his childhood, he always appeared alone.

He was a fat kid who wanted to be athletic but could not make the football team—or the choir. "Edwin, could you just mouth the words while the rest of us sing?" asked the choirmaster. In his early teens, he stole the family car and took it for a joy ride around the block. When he got back, his father was sitting on the front steps, his face unsmiling. His father on the lip of punishment is his story: no childhood friends, siblings, twin, or even mother people his stories. He was sent up to his room without supper, again and again scolded by his father until he truly starved himself, in his desperation to be thin, anorexia before we knew the word.

That he had a twin as an ally, a source of support or confusion, never entered his stories. She was, after all, a girl, and girls were useless, not part of the competition.

Still, Deane and I couldn't fathom that. If one of us were a boy, would it make a difference? We stare down at the photo: we are here because of them, our parents say. Twins run in families, every other generation, but we have twins in every one. Deane and I are relieved that we are not Buddy and Cissy. We prefer the identical Loves: a picture we understand. Seeing them, we know how the world sees us. As twins, we know how they see each other.

Our father has moved us from our grandmother's to a small house in Little Rock, Arkansas, where he works. Where Deane and I undo the household. "M's Foltz, all you do is dress those babies," says Artelia, a round black woman from a neighborhood we never see, who does everything else. For five dollars a week, she washes and irons the clothes, starching my father's shirts and my mother's white blouses. She flicks water at the iron and waits for it to spit back at her. The smell of soap and hot cloth and steam fill the kitchen. And then she starts to cook. She cooks dinner every night, firing an iron skillet so the cornbread sizzles when she pours the batter from the bowl. On Friday afternoons, she fries chicken, the legs and thighs piling up on an oval china platter. "Your supper's ready, M's Foltz," she says, changing her clothes, slipping back into heels and a hat she pins to the black hair coiled at the back of her head. In a bag she stuffs the gray dress she wears in our house, the headscarf that keeps the sweat and dust from her hair. My mother doesn't know where Artelia goes after work, or whom she returns to. At five, she walks to the bus stop on the corner where other black ladies stand and disappear.

All day, while Artelia cooks and cleans the house, our mother feeds and cleans us. Finished with one, she starts with the other. We eat every two hours, and our mother gets little sleep. Eventually, we stop throwing up and sleep three hours, then four. Our mother dresses in her best clothes, dresses us and puts us in a double carriage. She wheels us past the neighbors' houses. She wants the neighbors to see us, the rosebuds on the dresses she has made for us, the red, curly hair sprouting on our heads.

Here she knows no one, no one she is friends with. Our father is gone all day and cannot talk about his secret work. One day she follows him until he turns around, scolding her, "Go home, Deane. You know I can't tell you this stuff."

"You are no fun at all," she pouts, skillful as Lucy Ricardo denied her song and dance. "Why can't you? That Hoover can't even take a joke. And besides, there's no one to tell."

"I'll call you later. Maybe," growls my frowning father in his suit and fedora, repelled by a woman on his trail.

Our mother walks up one side of the street and down the other, hoping to bump into another mother. And then she goes home and starts all over, feeding, changing, bathing us. Every day our brother goes with her, dressed like a cowboy, his holster strapped to his waist. Every so often he sings her another verse of "Ragtime Cowboy Joe." "Out in Arizona where the bad men are, and the only friend to guide you is an evening star. The roughest, toughest man by far is Ragtime Cowboy Joe . . ."

He sings to her, but she cannot hear him. His sadness and loneliness, his singleness in a family of duos, is palpable. In pictures before we are born, he is always with our mother. In one, she sits laughing, one arm catching him around the waist, as if he is teasing her, pretending to pull away.

But now Deane and I are the center of attention, partly because we are miracles of repetition and people want to stare at us. But we are also dominating because we are sickly, and our precariousness makes us seem ephemeral. As if to answer expectations of doom, we develop throat infections. Our fevers go up and up. Our breathing knocks against the wall. At 2 a.m. our parents wrap blankets around us and rush us to the hospital. The nurses and doctors pump penicillin into our bottoms, and we become allergic to what can save us. Our father sits on the side of the bed and cries: he is sure we will die. Our tonsils swell, our throats close. As Uncle Tommy, a surgeon, carries us down to the operating room, we claw at his back, rasping. Our parents wait outside, drinking coffee and smoking while Jeff sleeps across a row of chairs. Tonight at least, we sound like elephants.

We recover and our weary mother sends us to nursery school. The first day she wakes us, our crisp, clean jumpers spread across the foot of the bed—the alert that we are going somewhere. In the kitchen we eat runny eggs and bacon while our mother hums at the skillet. We are going to nursery school, she says, but we don't know what she means. Our brother goes to school where he has to say, *Yes, ma'am,* where boys play on one side of the playground, girls on another, a chalked line dividing the two. Our mother bundles us into the car, and we park in front of a low brick building, and she walks us across its barren, dusty lot. Through the school's doors are strange adults, strange children, and lots of them. Nothing draws us except the real car parked in the playground. A dark-haired boy sits at the wheel turning and turning, driving in circles. This could get us somewhere. Deane climbs into the seat. The boy ignores her, speeding toward Kansas. "It's my turn," says Deane. He spins on. She leans over and shoves her hand into his curls and pulls. "It's my TURN."

The teachers come running, lift down the crying boy, then Deane and me. They take us inside and seat Deane, her face to the corner. I have to sit with brackish canned orange juice and graham crackers, and I won't eat them. I sneak over to Deane, sit next to her. "I'm sitting here too," I say over the fingers I am sucking. And she stops crying. I too am in the corner, where the bad kids go, where mistakes happen. But the teachers come and get me. *You can't see her.* The fear sloshes in my stomach like soup. I hate the curly-haired boy and the teachers and the canned orange juice. The sorrow I feel is also knowledge: what happens to Deane happens to me. I know this the way I know my hair is red and my eyes are blue. What I don't yet know is that this link between us is not universal, not something everyone gets to have.

Chapter 7

My sister did not die for eight more days, although her brain died the moment she was shot. That first morning, we return to the hospital and the nurses have moved her out of a private room into intensive care, and when we tiptoe in to see her, we find ourselves in public, with other dying or gravely ill patients and their families, each patient separated by gauzy curtains and the machines that pump out life. I walk down the hall to see Deane, although I am unable to speak to her in front of strangers. The intensive care unit, despite its opaque separations, is crowded and chairless like a small grocery where people have to turn sideways to get past each other, the steady beat of machines, the Musak. My mother follows me and, strangely, this angers me, even in this space where privacy is not possible. I am so mad, I cannot breathe. And for that moment, Deane seems unreachable. My mother sees my spurt of rage and turns back. But I am dead to her sorrow, to anyone's sorrow but the dry space newly mine. I stand by Deane, holding her hand, watching her face, wondering how I can fall into whatever space she has retreated to. Her silence is a script I read, and we leave our mother as we always have. When I walk back, my mother sits in our hospital room, turned away from me. Together we move back into the dead, impartial air.

That afternoon, my brother arrives, and when he sees my face, he too knows what we wait for. My face, he recalls, "a thousand miles of desperation."

"It said, 'Tell me what I can do, even though there is nothing,'" Jeff tells me years later. Jeff is six-foot-two, with a rower's body and a face like

Robert Redford's. His good looks and strong posture are what anyone notices first, remarks on first. Unlike my dad, he never wears a tie. He sits beside my mother, lifts her hand into his, asks me to sit on his other side.

"What are they saying?" he asks.

"We haven't seen the surgeon yet," answers my father. My brother has always been our champion, the one who protected Deane and me on the playground. But I don't know him, really: he left for college when we were thirteen, and he was married by his senior year with a daughter the year after that. He is most like our mother—sensitive, easily hurt, with a long memory and a big temper. But he is like Dad too: it is too hard for Jeff to be powerless to change what can't be.

The rest of the floor where we have our room remains void of patients. Perhaps hospital personnel have isolated us because my sister's killer is still at large. But this is not a question we articulate. Instead we greet the countless people—Deane's friends and colleagues—who have the courage to face our blank, white sorrow. For we are ghosts ourselves, almost without affect, dry and silent. We have phone calls to make, although I remember few of them. When do I learn to say, *Hello, my sister is dying?*

She has been shot, and she is dying. I tell the story over and over, call people who have not heard from me in years, their voices joyful, then withering to silence when I say the words. After one of these calls, I lie down in a separate room, away from the others, on a stiff hospital bed, and look at the blue that fills the window, the sunny sky, the edgy New England weather. I am struck by its persistence. What can I do with such a bright day, when death sits in its middle? I want a bruised sky. But what I see is the sky's survival. What I see is that nothing will stop except my sister.

The flowers pour in until our sitting room is full. *To the Foltz family.* Deane's friends crowd in as well and spill into the hallway. Many people I have never met, her colleagues who know Deane's death might have been theirs. They recognize me without introduction. As they approach me, their faces wince and all that these people understand of sorrow and luck lies open for me to see. Although they are strangers, we are oddly intimate. I am their chance to say goodbye, to see Deane one more time, to get as close to her as they can get. Once they say their names, I recognize them in turn, the people Deane told me about.

Deane's best friend, Sarah, arrives with her husband, Gary. I see on her face the disbelief and exhaustion I too feel. Sarah has a long, pale face that carries sadness, even when she smiles. I was always jealous of Deane's friendship with Sarah, that she had found someone to be so close to, someone so different from me, someone I don't know.

"Oh, Sarah," I say as we hug.

"Doe," she says my nickname in her low, husky voice. I know that like me, she has no one like Deane.

"Where's Emi?" I ask about her one-year-old daughter.

"She's fine," she says. "At a friend's."

My mother leans in to ask her questions about Emi, to keep the patter going. This is her role now, a part I have no interest in. Rudeness, in this new world, is a new exemption.

I have not eaten for twenty-four hours. Food seems like nonsense, an affront. But I also do not feel well. We walk to the hospital's underground cafeteria for food. I watch the people come and go, wondering what their stories are, whom they are losing upstairs. I order a bowl of chowder and dip my spoon in. But when I taste the salty cream, I also remember Deane, and swallowing becomes something I used to do.

We have yet to see a doctor, but today, day two, the nurses say one is coming. He is a brain surgeon who meets with us in an empty hospital room. I look closely to memorize the face of the man who let my sister go unhealed. He has dark eyes and hair, and he is brief.

"The back of your daughter's head was hit by a .357 magnum bullet."

We stare at him, waiting.

"Is there any hope?"

"A .357 can destroy the engine of a car. If we take her off the respirator she will die."

"Did she know. . . . Did she feel anything?"

"Her brain died instantly."

"But her hands and feet . . . they move."

"Her movements now are like the movements of a chicken with its head cut off."

We already hate him, but that ugly sentence makes us wonder what news he thinks he is delivering. He stares back at us, as if he is bewildered by our anger. That night we go to a restaurant for dinner—my family; Deane's husband, Art; her best friend, Sarah, and husband, Gary.

"What did you think of the doctor?" my mother asks me down the long table.

"He is a dirty fucker," I answer, and my Southern mother, who has never carried fuck, even close to her beautiful lips, smiles at me.

Art is smiling too, his brown flop of hair falling over his forehead. He wants to stay near Deane, and so my brother has offered him the spare bed in his motel room. In our crisis, none of us think about Deane and Art's dissolving marriage, that they are midway through a divorce. Art has always been easy to be around; he is now, too. Like my husband, Danny, he is quiet and unassuming, quick to offer help or simply do a task without asking. He still lives in the Tufts dormitory where he and Deane had been house parents, a job that allows him time to do his painting.

"What will you do?" he asks me.

"I need to go to her apartment to get some clothes," I say. "I'm cold."

He nods and puts his arm around my shoulder. "I could take you."

"Danny's going to drive Mom and Dad's rental." He nods, his brown eyes moist behind his wire-frame glasses. He takes them off to rub his eyes, wipes the glasses on his napkin.

I feel sorry for him, not yet angry. But I also realize I don't want to go into Deane's house with him, where she has scratched out her married name and written *Foltz*. I shopped with her as she pulled herself into a new life without him, buying a rug, bookshelves, a wall hanging. How hard it must be for him to be here, now outside Deane's life. But none of us care about that at this moment. My parents know nothing of his affair and little about the reasons for their separation, that Deane felt weighted by his sadness, the legacy of abandonment by his father when Art was a young boy.

"I can't have children with him," she told me. "I can't see him as a father. I would be taking care of them all."

It wasn't his affair with an art graduate student that made her leave. But it informed her: she saw more clearly that this wasn't a man she could build a life with no matter how she loved him, and she did. She had worked to protect Art, his privacy, even as she left him. And they are still bound by the house they were trying to sell, by the marriage in limbo. We do what Deane would want and bring him in.

A twin who marries has two spouses, the fact an undertow tearing at a marriage. But Art too had his own undertow. For a long time, Deane knocked at his windows, peering in, looking for a man who could say how much he loved her. What she had taken for his quiet was something more serious, a numbing grief that silenced him. After six years he found another woman. Deane moved into a friend's unheated apartment and filed for divorce. Intimacy is not simple for a twin. But recognizing its absence is a twin's specialty.

By Monday, I have developed a case of poison ivy, picked up the day before my sister was shot, as I trimmed the hedge, readying my yard in Tennessee for her visit. My sister would not care about the hedge, but clipping seemed to bring her sooner. I didn't see the poison growing among the leaves. So I too go to the emergency room, to the same doctors and nurses who had cared for my sister only three days ago. *Yes, you look just like her*, they tell me. Already I love any word of her, any connection I make to those who saw her, who know what happened to her, who tried to save her. They feel it, too. They like seeing me, to help her. But I hate being there. My own body is beside the point; poison ivy is nothing, an embarrassment. And yet the poison keeps pumping into my reddened face. The medics give me a shot and prescribe ointment, and they talk to me about Deane. They regard me with sorrow, but they are skilled at death and loss, and so they also let me see a simple happiness: their pleasure in how much we look alike. They were the last to see it. They fetch me her ruined clothes. I look into the bag and realize these clothes are as changed as her face, so darkened with blood I cannot recognize them. I throw the bag away.

I go to a drugstore near the hospital to get the ointment. The clerk smiles, asks me how it's going, makes a joke about poison ivy, the crisp weather. I am supposed to say something, but I can't. I can only speak in a tongue that will make me seem crazy. I am glad to climb back into the car with my mother and father and Dan, where it is normal for life to be unspeakable.

Chapter 8

Deane and I are so alike that we have trouble identifying ourselves in photos, scrawling our guesses over our heads in crayon. In home movies, our heads are often turned the same way, the curls frilling our necks at the same slant. We trot back and forth like blurred film, one set of duplicate images, chattering, fluent in our private language. About 40 percent of all twins have one—a phenomenon linguists call *cryptophasia* or *idioglossia*. We are slow in speaking English—common among premature twins—but we have plenty of twin words. We babble with intent, one speaking, the other listening.

From the start our mother dresses us alike, buys matching dresses for herself. Twins are an attraction to emphasize, like two exclamation marks. After all, we were born in the pre-fertilization '50s. Without artificial means, only four births per thousand are twins, and two-thirds of those are fraternal. (Today, twins—identical and fraternal—make up thirty-two of every one thousand births, although the natural rate remains the same.) We are a rarity, the only identical twins my parents know, and both love showing us off. Mother-daughter dresses are the fashion, regardless of whether a mother has twins. Patternmakers like Simplicity and Butterick sell mother-daughter patterns, and some companies hire housewives to go door to door with "style cards," offering mother-daughter patterns, a swatch of material attached. Deane and I make our mother fashionable.

Deane and I sleep in the same room, the round turret room of an old house in Shaker Heights, Ohio, since our father now negotiates labor relations for a Cleveland manufacturing company, Borg-Warner. We share dolls, sitting on the wooden stairs stuffing cheese in their perpetually open mouths, and letting it dry a cracked yellow. We lie on the floor together with our brother watching our first TV, our chins propped on our palms. On Christmas morning we run down the stairs, and in the living room is a doll bed for our cheesy dolls but big enough for us to lie in. We climb into the tight space and watch snow fall outside the windows. Cleveland freezes us in.

But we are not in Cleveland long. Our father takes a job in Camden, New Jersey, with Campbell Soup Company. Before they offer him the job, the executives (nicknamed by my father "men of measured merriment," a phrase from Sinclair Lewis's novel *Arrowsmith*) ask to meet our mother.

"Deane, don't say a word in the meeting," our father tells her, his left eyebrow raised in warning. "I'll do all the talking." He is, after all, a man raised by a critical father who dominated the household, his mother a shadowy figure my father never told one story about.

Our red-haired mother, standing by the stove, stares at him, poking his egg with a fork before she turns it, shrinking into her silent treatment.

"Here're your eggs, if that's not too much for me to say."

"Deanie, this is business," Dad says, his hand hovering over his plate. "It's just better not to say anything." He is both certain that he will fail the interview and determined in a lock-jawed way that he will, by God, get the job. But in his insecurity, he sees in my mother his own failings. And he lives in a society where ideas are dominated by men. He is proud of my mother's beauty, her social warmth, her intense interest in other people, the way she leans forward when they are talking, the way she asks questions, opening her listener to her experience as well. But a business meeting—that's his province.

"Do you want the dry cleaning picked up today? Not that I want to say anything. I won't even speak if they ask me to."

"Mitch," he sighs. "Yes, the cleaning would be good." He wipes the yolk off his face and puts his brown hat on. "I'm off."

Our mother doesn't turn around until she hears the door shut. "Good," she says.

On moving day, the turret house empties. My father takes me to breakfast, and my mother takes Deane and Jeff, the first separation I remember. Dad and I order a stack of pancakes that arrive under a silver dome. I am thrilled to have him to myself, but I also wonder where Deane is, what she is doing. It is sweeter thinking of her reaction than acknowledging my own. Because until I tell her something, nothing has happened.

"Deane." I race toward her, holding out the pack of peanut butter crackers Dad bought me. "Look what Daddy bought me."

"Mommy got us this," Deane says, holding up a pinwheel. She hands it to me, shows me how to blow on it so the wheel turns, blurring the colors.

"Here." I hand her a cracker. "Let's eat it fast. The first one to whistle gets another one." We sit on the steps, filling our mouths with peanut butter crackers, blowing cracker crumbs on the sidewalk as we whistle. "I win," we both shout. And I give her another one.

In Gladwyne, suburban Philadelphia, we pull up to the white brick house Dad bought, one even our mother has never seen. It's big, in the middle of a hill that keeps on going into a huge field bordered by woods. Up the block lies an enormous water tower that will surely burst, drowning us all. While our parents explore the house and Jeff scouts the yard, Deane and I stand in the back of a station wagon eating white meringues out of a cookie tin. Soon our mother and father come out of the new house and carry us in, our mouths beaded with sugar. Deane and I love the house from the minute we walk in. They lift us up and sweep us into a white kitchen, a white Formica table at the center of an empty room. We are home now, my mother says, and sets out bowls of tomato soup and saltines for supper. She puts candles on the table and turns out the lights. Deane and I watch each other's faces wobble through the candles' flame.

For our father, the move is a shift into financial success. Ever since his father had hauled him out of college because he had made the lowest grades of the four siblings, his ambitions were stoked by that smoldering humiliation. When my mother visited him at Washington and Lee, he'd haul her to the bulletin board where grades were posted, certain he'd failed, relieved he hadn't. On blank afternoons, he'd walk into the nearby Virginia Hills, staring at House Mountain while he wondered what would become of him. One older brother was a businessman, another a doctor. Law was what was left to the son of a doctor with the largest library in Fort Smith. "Ssssslander," he'd whisper into our ears, teaching us his legal jargon when we were little. "Liiiiibel," he'd say, pretending to scribble on a pad.

After law school, he got a clerkship in Washington, DC, above an FBI office, and soon, with World War II coming, it was easy for the agents to recruit him to the floor below. He'd done everything from delivering dry cleaning to John Edgar Hoover to chasing German spies in taxis he commandeered from terrified college girls. (After he handcuffed the spy and handed him off to colleagues, he returned the girls to their dorm, walking them in to face the horrified, elderly housemother.) At our birth, he was agent-in-charge in Little Rock, Arkansas. But he soon realized that an FBI salary wouldn't educate three children. A former colleague recruited by Borg-Warner to conduct labor negotiations knew G-men could play hard and went after my dad, opening a wide avenue for his ambitions.

From this new house, we have to go to school, a building made of bulging gray stones, dark and jagged like stones dragons climb over. We walk down the hall full of dark paintings of Bambi and Thumper staring at us, somber as Rembrandts. Our mother leads us into a room filled with sprawling children hiding behind partitions and lying about on desks. They are thugs who need to wipe their noses and button their shirts. But we stay. And this day, our mother stays too.

The children stare at us. Not because we are new, but because we are one person split in half, mirrors not one of them has seen before. Born decades before in-vitro fertilization, we are the school's only set of twins, a kindergarten sideshow. The principal sees no reason to separate us, and so like our faces, our school lives are identical: the books we use, the friends we make, the boys we kiss.

Brown-haired Ray slides on his butt behind the class partition, leaning his pasty face toward mine for a smooch. Today is our birthday, and our mother has brought the class a cake.

"Wanna kiss?" he says, as if he's asking me if I want a sip of water.

"I will if you wipe your nose," I answer. I scoot toward him too, my skirt around my knees. We do a movie star kiss, grinding our faces like we see in the movies. He scoots toward Deane. "Wanna kiss," he begins again.

Deane and I are a unit, and our classmates treat us that way. In class pictures, Deane's knees spread her skirt open like an umbrella, and mine do too, our loafers splayed like frog's feet, our elbows on the desk, our fingers braided, our bodies set identically as if we've been arranged, told how to sit. Except the other children slump and twist, each one apart, no dice roll of two.

Our mother picks us up at noon and after lunch, we nap. Or rather, Deane and I play doctor, poking about in our underwear determined to see on each other what we can't see on ourselves. Our mother comes back into the room as I am bending over Deane giving her a look-see.

"Ohohohnonono girls," stutters our mother, shaking her head of curls. "You mustn't do that. People don't look at each other's tooties."

"Why, Mommy?" we ask in unison, a choir of ignorance.

"You keep your panties on, and you don't let other people see. Nice people don't do that." Our mother has her glasses on, enlarging her frown.

"We won't, Mommy," Deane agrees. "We won't."

"Go to sleep," says our mother, tucking our pink and blue blankets under our chins. The door closes.

Lying there, we wonder at the dark gummy sides of ourselves, the holes and the filters. These are mysteries our mother is not gifted at explaining. She is talented instead at spreading a nebulous haze of worry toward our bodies. They are trouble—and not nice or right. But Deane's body answers questions about mine. What I see on her is only what I know myself to be.

That night we throw blankets over chairs in our bedroom and crawl into the tent with baby dolls. It is dark here and throughout the house. The murmur of our parents' voices has stopped, and I crawl back up on my bed and lie down with my head facing the window. And then I hear a choking sound—Deane on the next bed, crying into her pillow. I climb out of my bed and go to hers. She pulls the covers back so I can get in. I lie next to her. I turn on my side and put my fingers out, touching her face, her tears.

At our birthday party, our mother had run out of cake slices. The plates had been passed around the desks to Hutchie and Karen, to Ricky and Pamela, and when our turn came, there were no more pieces. When our mother saw our disappointed faces, she pushed her red lips together and shook her head.

I do not know whether Deane is crying over the cake or our mother's angry lips. But I talk about what we will do tomorrow. I make her promise to wake me when she wakes up, and we will put on holsters for our cap guns and bridle our stick horses or catch the black dog to ride. *Catch the black dog?* she asks, pulling her fingers out of her mouth long enough to get this out. The neighborhood dogs are disguised horses living on Black Rock Road entirely for our purposes. We gather them with ropes and leashes and trot behind them through the neighbors' yards, over the fences until we reach the tire swing at the heart of the woods. We tie our dog-horses and climb up the high log, the launch for the tire swing. I go first, swinging into the space of clouds and trees. I am sending my glee into the woods where no one hears me but Deane. *We'll do that again*, I tell her.

I have her attention. And I get her to do what is essential: I get her to stop crying—because her pain is unbearable.

Chapter 9

Outside in a world I barely attend, the Lowell police scramble to find James Palmer. Minutes after the shooting, the police go to Palmer's house. His wife tells them Palmer left just twenty minutes before to buy fertilizer.

Fertilizer.

They tell her he has shot someone. She is distraught, dumbfounded, and pregnant, her eighteen-month-old daughter on her hip. They take her to Palmer's mother, who has talked with James just this morning, just family conversation, that's all.

All day Friday, the police interview the people who were at Stoney Brook. Nancy, the office manager, tells police that Palmer's last visit was in June: "He was a very agitated person," she says. She remembers his bursting in without an appointment, asking to see a therapist NOW. "But I don't want to see Deane," he says. "I want to see Alan Shields."

On Friday, someone spots him near a racquetball center called The Courthouse. Others, hearing the police scanner, confuse that: they think he is hiding in the Lowell District Court. Cruisers surround the building. Workers spill onto the street, all but one entrance sealed. Eventually, police realize both leads are useless. Still, uneasy, they check everyone reentering the courthouse for weapons.

One hundred police plus the people who work for Safeguard, the security company where Palmer works as a guard, search for a blue Datsun with a red stripe and the inscription Industrial Security. "The car should stick out like a sore thumb," says an officer. On highways, drivers spot Palmer's blue Datsun everywhere, besieging police with false leads.

On Saturday an anonymous caller tells the police Palmer is drinking at a bar on Route 3A in Billerica, Massachusetts, about seven miles from Lowell. Billerica officers surround the bar while plainclothesmen enter to find neither Palmer nor the caller.

On Monday, officers swarm a ringer car on the street. But it's only a duplicate member of the Safeguard fleet. The police ask the company to pull its red-striped duplicates off the road.

These are called *unsuccessful stakeouts.* The Chelmsford police chief Raymond McKeon, who knows Palmer, who knew his dead father, has slept four hours since Friday. Knowing them, he says, that makes it hard.

The headlines, the broadcasts are full of Palmer, of manhunts, of searching, of his photo, wire to wire, station to station. *A massive dragnet*, they call it. The director of Stoney Brook, Roger Coleman, appears in front of the center.

"Unlikely town, unlikely place, unlikely people. . . . It was a one-in-a-million shot," he says as police fan out across the city, the state, the next state. The center offers a $5,000 reward for Palmer's capture. Bullet-vested police—a small army— surround Palmer's home on a quiet street of eight houses. All night they lie inside the darkened house. Waiting for what? For him to sneak back in, to lie down, to feel safe?

He and his wife, Debbie, built the brown cape-style house with yellow shutters, the yard bare, PALMER 16 on the mailbox. A nice couple, his neighbors say. Nice neighbors. A man who came out to mow his grass. They just didn't bother anyone.

Divers comb the quarry where someone saw Palmer drive after the shooting. Helicopters fly overhead, twice swooping down on men mistaken for Palmer. Police on motorcycles ride on small lanes, into the deep woods, past ponds and more quarries. The police call in the FBI. They check the airports, motels, bank accounts. The car has vanished, they say, probably deep in the New England woods or at the bottom of a lake.

Pranksters call the police: he's at a Holiday Inn, he's at a tennis club. On Wednesday and Thursday, planes and helicopters fly like cowboys anxious to throw a lasso—and Friday they stop, after a fruitless scour. They hunt down a sighting, stalking railroad tracks until they find a teenage boy eating grapes. A man pretends he knows where Palmer is to impress his girlfriend, to get back at a woman who's dropped him.

The Chelmsford police send a "wanted" notice to Arizona state police. They know Palmer had gone there the year before and also Los Angeles, where he took a police exam in September.

"He should be considered armed and dangerous," reads the notice. They send notices to the Boston & Maine Railroad Police.

"There's no rhyme nor reason to this one," says one cop. "It's a pig in a poke now."

Sometimes when I am reinventing August 14, I imagine Palmer's mother barren. I imagine a world without Palmer. But Palmer, a reserve police officer and security guard, the son of a former Chelmsford chief of police, is still roving out there in a car with guns. I picture him on a highway in New Hampshire, pulling off at a McDonald's. The restaurant is full, and everyone eats burgers with a murderer. But more surprising than my fantasies is how much he doesn't matter—unless finding him, I could push him backward, roll him over August 14, slide him onto August 13, and plug him there, a stopped life.

After the murders, one tipster said he saw Palmer at a bar: scotch on the rocks.

He doesn't matter. He's all that matters.

Chapter 10

In 1954, when Deane and I are five and Jeff ten, the trip by train from Philadelphia to Fort Smith, Arkansas, where our grandparents live, takes three nights and two days. Our father, who is busy and can't go, kisses us and shepherds us up the iron stairs of the *Spirit of St. Louis*, where a porter collects us and leads us to the Pullman car. In a compartment of chairs that turn into beds, my mother tips the porter, thanking him with the reserve she saves for men, especially black men, who are strangers.

Mom, Jeff, Deane, and I are leaving for the whole of a smothering July while our father continues to work in Philadelphia. This is a journey we make only two or three times in our childhood. Our father has begun to insist on renting a house every July in Stone Harbor, New Jersey, not my mother's idea of the foreign adventures she longed for—although she does give up cooking and shopping for the month, letting our father wield the grocery cart, filling it with what he calls "rat's cheddar" and Ritz crackers. After our grandfather dies, our grandmother comes east, staying for weeks with us and then for weeks in Wilmington, Delaware, where her other daughter lives.

The train jerks forward and we wind to the dining car of white-clothed tables where black waiters in starched white jackets carry trays topped with silver domes. One seats us at a table, and as my mother orders, we stare out the window, the scenery of our meal shifting wheat field by wheat field. We turn in our seats to stare at the boy behind us.

"I'm related to Elvis Presley," he informs us.

My brother pulls his yo-yo out of his pocket, does a spin to the floor, and then shoots it horizontally toward the boy, who doesn't flinch.

"I am," he insists before his father turns his shoulders back to the table.

Our mother's shrimp cocktail arrives in a glass dish, the shrimp hanging over its side like jumpers. She obliges them slowly, eating each shrimp in eight bites, like no one has anything else in the world to do but eat—or wait for her to eat. She chews tiny bites like a star in a movie, her full lips transferring their beauty, and we want shrimp too. But our domed plates arrive, the waiter lifts the covers, and underneath mine are two sausages thick as cigars. The grease glistens on the skin, and I am going to throw up.

My mother guides me through the car to the bathroom. She stands behind me, one hand on my stomach, the other cool on my forehead, and together we lean over the toilet. If it is possible to feel safe while gagging, I do. She is not mad at leaving her Crown Royal and shrimp, and when we stagger back to the dining car, she orders me ginger ale and pretzels. She knows illness, understands it like other mothers understand brownies or chocolate chip cookies. It is her specialty, turning illness into privilege, into some strange reprieve of happiness.

When we go back to our Pullman, the porter has unlocked the berths, and four beds hang from the walls. The train's perpetual shimmy puts us to sleep, but in the middle of the night, the shimmy stops. Men, women, porters scurry past our window on a platform, and I am sleeping next to the world. I swing my head over the side.

"Deane."

She looks outside, then climbs into my berth, and we lie together, laughing at people in raincoats who pass but don't see us.

The next day, during the layover in St. Louis, we climb into the echoing station and onto the city sidewalks. Our mother holds our hands and has Jeff walk just ahead. A man staggers toward us on the sidewalk.

"Change, ma'am?" he asks, opening his mouth to demonstrate to us that some grown-ups have few teeth, and those are yellow. Our mother's arms embrace our shoulders, and she answers by cutting past, moving forward as if she knows where she's going. Only when we dip inside a restaurant does she relax her grip.

One side of the restaurant is covered in compartments like post-office box windows, and behind each glass square rests a slice of pie, sandwich, or chocolate milk. Our mother swings open the doors to orange cupcakes, their icing peeling off like a book cover.

"After this," she says, "we'll go to the zoo, where they have an elephant named Dorothy."

Near us sit enormous fat people, their table piled with food. Deane and I look at their stomachs hanging between their knees, and orange cupcakes don't seem so much fun anymore. It scares us that people could be that fat, that we could be that fat. Two-ton sisters.

When we pull into the station at Fort Smith, Dottie, our grandmother, stands on the platform, huge and unsmiling, wearing a pink linen dress and black-and-white spectator shoes. She has a flat, wide body, spread hips, and broad shoulders, and she is glad to get in a fight with anyone.

"Porter," she says, pointing her white-gloved hand at our bags.

We climb into the Arkansas heat and thrust our faces into her wide, soft stomach, a good start.

Our grandmother hands the porter a fifty-cent piece while we wait in her car. Her car has air-conditioning—something we don't have in our Philadelphia cars—and its flat, fake air removes us from the shimmering heat that fries Fort Smith. It is like riding in the pink gum bubbles we pop from our mouths. We drive through downtown and the streets are empty of anything but glare, the noontime cafeterias shut, the theatre marquee lights out, the box office glass down. We turn into neighborhoods of big houses with white columns and sleeping porches set behind sprawling oak trees. Gradually the houses and even the trees grow smaller, closer together, closer to the shrinking roads, until we turn onto our grandmother's street, a double row of single-story brick houses, box hedges, and purple hydrangea. The identical houses sit close together, a row of hats along a shelf.

That night we pummel Mom with questions, wanting to imagine her little-girl self in the same beds we sleep in. She tells us stories of Sunday afternoon rides with her parents to pick up homemade potato chips. As she remembers them, she licked her lips as if the tiny crystals of salt remained, and all we want at that moment is to crunch those chips and ride with her in an open-top car on the dirt roads near Fort Smith. She tells us of the way our grandmother once pinned a sixteen-year-old bully to a classroom wall in the St. Louis school where she was principal before she met our grandfather Harry. Deane and I wriggle farther down under our covers, delighted by our champion grandmother.

But there is a darker tale her mother spreads, and our mother spreads to us: the world, it seems, is full of danger, particularly from men. She tells us of black men who come to the front door only to get a tongue lashing from our grandmother.

"How dare you come to the front," she says to the graying man who stands back from the door, his cap in hand. "You get to the back, and then I'll talk to you."

"Ahright, Miz Mitchell. I didn't mean anything, Miz Mitchell," the man says, turning slowly back down the steps. Blacks were a worry to my grandmother, who wanted their yard work or their fresh fish or vegetables they sometimes brought door to door. But they were ominous entries from a part of town we should never see. Blacks were a shakily controlled menace, the scariest of all those men after white ladies.

Our mother absorbed the fear, cut thick by her mother, so that as she moved into adulthood, the world remained a child's haunted vision. Underpinning my mom's fears was her mother's fury at her husband, Harry. A gentle alcoholic, a dry goods salesman who traveled through the state from store to store, he also stayed past the trip's confines, disappearing for days to drink without his stern fundamentalist wife staring back at him.

Our mother doesn't tell these stories: she talks about how much Harry loves cards and horse races and buttermilk with crushed saltines. Her father is the soft spot in the house. While we are visiting, he teaches us to shuffle cards and lets us spin his automatic shuffler as if we couldn't break it. He says using the machine is cheating, and he cuts the deck and cups one half in each hand, pressing his index finger down on the deck's center, letting his thumb slide bottom to top so the cards alternate like marching cadets back into formation. When we try it, the cards fly all over the floor.

When it was time for college, Mom said, her parents gave her a wardrobe of dresses and an allowance of five cents a week, enough for a Coca-Cola with her friends. We stared at our Coca-Cola–loving mother, who drank one every morning with her coffee, and tried to imagine waiting a whole week for something so sweet.

The mantel in the living room is covered with pecan-filled cakes and cheesy casseroles, ham and green beans covered with glass lids. In Fort Smith, family visitors get the same treatment as the dead: a room full of homemade foods. Our grandmother's friends keep coming up the steps like caterers. Our grandmother steps out on the porch, our mother behind her, her voice rising to high enthusiasm. The friends come inside and stand, able to talk and talk until our bones ache with boredom. We drop to all fours and crawl until our heads bump Mrs. Green's long skirts that drape on our heads like veils, and we rotate our heads under her skirts and look up into the white bloom of her panties.

"Girls, you come out from there," says our mother. Mrs. Green smooths her skirts and smiles down at us. But her cheeks have reddened in patches, and she is backing toward the door.

Our mother marches us into the middle bedroom, her fingers pressing into our arms, and sits on the bed. She bends Deane over her knee and swats her on the bottom, then lifts me up to do the same.

"You girls do not look up ladies' dresses."

My bottom stings long after she leaves, and I lie down on the bed next to Deane, sucking my middle fingers as Deane is, her tears working their way down her cheeks. Our foreheads touch, and we pull the sheet up over our heads.

"Did you see her underpants?" I ask.

Summer mornings in the South are a narcotic. The air shimmers, and a truck with a scoop could gather heat. The male cicadas buzz into their romances. Deane and I play on our grandmother's sidewalk, drawing a hopscotch board with chalk. Once I've reached box eight and back to one without tipping over, I'm done and happy to be done. Deane jumps through the hopscotch boxes, leaning down to pick up the stone she's thrown. When she stands up, her dress has risen on her stomach, its waist like a ribbon tied around the center of a ball. Soon my mother, sleek in green linen, comes out on the porch. Deane hops toward her, but her foot slips on the first porch step, kicking out so that her head falls forward. Her open mouth lands on the stair above, her left front tooth slamming into concrete, and in one wild rush, instead of playing hopscotch, we are in the car going to the dentist.

She does not lose her tooth. But within a week her tooth has turned black like the tooth of a pirate. When she smiles, a spot of darkness tells everyone who Deane is. I envy her the tooth, and I peer into her mouth for its secret. She takes the tooth in her fingers and wiggles it back and forth.

"Stop that, Deanie," says our mother. "You have to keep the tooth until the next one comes in."

We sit in our grandmother's kitchen, staring at the silver tub on the floor. Our mother has told us to stay at the table and eat our crustless peanut butter sandwiches. But when she leaves, we crouch down to the tub. In the clouding water is an enormous catfish, its long whiskers brushing the silver as it turns. Paul, our grandmother's black gardener, has come to the back door this morning, hoisting the tub. Our brother goes in the yard for a stick, ties string on the end, and dangles it over the catfish's head. The freckles, the blubber lips, the tentacle whiskers are magnified in the water. Deane and I kneel down and put our faces close until the fish thuds his tail against the bucket. Deane's black tooth is nothing next to this black part of the river.

Finally, our grandmother takes a net and lifts the catfish out of the water and carries it to her white sink. She and Mom stare down at the fish and discuss where the hammer is, but neither of them moves. The catfish's mouth opens and closes like someone about to answer them, changing his mind over and over, until his mouth stays closed. My grandmother blows a big sigh through her pursed lips and hauls the catfish back out on the counter. She takes a knife from the drawer, and our mother hustles us into the living room. That night we eat catfish strips and cornpone and coleslaw. The catfish strips taste crispy and salty and tinny. We want Paul to come back with another fish in a pool. But Dottie says he won't, not if she can help it. Still, she eats more catfish than anyone.

After dinner, we jump on the beds so I land when Deane rises. Outside the window the hydrangeas rise and fall too. We can see Jackie, our neighbor, through her window, so close we could bridge our bodies from our window to hers. But our mother comes back, insists that we lie down on the white sheets that stick to our skin. The heat settles over our bodies like a blanket, and the drone of cicadas fills whatever the air's missing.

Most days we go swimming at the Hardscrabble Country Club in a huge pool where only white children swim. On the way to Hardscrabble we pass a community pool filled with black children. Our mother explains you have to "belong" to Hardscrabble to swim there. Deane and I stand on the side waiting to jump when a boy comes up from behind and pushes me in.

"Northern scaredy cat," he laughs. "Where's your mama?"

"You are a big jerk," Deane says as he moves toward her.

"I don't see but one jerk," he smiles, his hands outstretched.

When I come up, I see the teeth in that smile, the slightly crooked one that pushes in front of the rest, that pushes his lip out. He takes a step toward Deane.

"You stop there, buster." My grandmother comes over to the side. "Where's your mother, you ill-mannered boy?" she asks, the principal resurrecting.

He stares at the ground and shrugs, rubbing his big toe over the concrete, then points to a girl in a chair, no longer Mr. Big Stuff.

"That's my sister," he says, his lip trembling.

My grandmother takes the boy by the arm and leads him to his sister. "He pushed my granddaughter in," she says. "Where's your mother? I don't want to see him in the pool again today."

My sister and I cross to the other side and decide to speak to each other under water. We jump up and down to get momentum and then plunge to the bottom, our legs folded as if we were in a campfire circle, and lean toward each other.

"I hate him," Deane says, her bubbly words gurgling toward me, and we surge back up to the surface.

"Big scab," I say back to her, and she nods. We plunge back down. When we come up, we take turns floating. I put my arms under Deane's back, two braces, and float her around, a human raft. I see my grandmother and mother sitting in chairs by the pool. My grandmother has a pink chiffon scarf around her head, and she's staring toward the bully corner.

Deane and I climb out and sit on towels in front of our mother and play. We watch the boy, who sits on a towel glaring at us. We know boys like this at school, who fight by grabbing each other's penises, squeezing. They turn on each other like the dogs that fight in our yard. Deane and I want to tell someone. When we tell our mother, she says to tell our teacher. Which of course is impossible. Afterward, the boy who cries seems ruined, like collapsed clay. Deane and I want to say something to him, but boys—these boys—can't talk this way. The playground sickens with sweat and sometimes blood and always this salty defeat.

We jump back into the water, away from him, away from his friends who look so mean they must have grown up on dirt roads, without mothers. From our corners we watch them dunk and splash each other. One boy holds another's head under until we think his neck will snap, and when he comes up he pulls in the air as if it is a milkshake.

That summer we are baptized. We have not yet been taken under Heaven's wing—so our mother says. She dresses us in pinafores covered with pink roses, and we go in the side door of the yellow brick church, our grandmother first, into the reverend's office where we change into swimsuits. We are heartened until Dottie and Mom leave us alone with the Reverend. He doesn't get in a swimsuit. He takes off his shoes and socks and rolls up the trousers beneath the black robe that dips to his ankles. He opens a door of his office and motions us through. Inside, a pool takes up the room as if someone forgot the deck and beach chairs and umbrellas. The Reverend takes our hands, and we wade into the warm water. Curtains open at the far wall, and there again are our mother and Dottie and every single person in the whole church and their eyeballs times two. The reverend takes my hand.

"Hold your nose," he says, and placing his other hand on the small of my back, he dips me backward until my head breaks through the water.

"Christ claims you for his own," he says, rubbing my forehead. "Receive the sign of his cross."

When he is sure I am completely wet, he pulls me up again and motions me to the side and restarts with Deane, who is sucking both her middle fingers, even as he dips.

"Do not be ashamed to confess the faith of Christ crucified."

Our grandmother and mother are crying, and then we are sloshing back toward the reverend's office. Although we are no longer sinners, it is the worst swim we have ever had.

We stay in Fort Smith until the air turns cold, at least at night. Our grandmother has a furnace that shoots its heat through a floor grid. Our mother warns us to step around the grid, and we think of it as a pit with a dragon. We drop pennies through its squares, counting *one two* until we hear them land. We stare down to see what red tongues appear. The gas cuts in and out, the monster's breath, so hot we pull our hands back.

On Sundays we wear organdy dresses and black patent leather shoes. Our Aunt Jo takes us on a trolley to buy Mary Janes. We eat salty crackers and carry our shoeboxes under our arms. When we get home, we put on our new shoes to show our mother. Deane scoots out of the room, across the polished floors, sliding feet first like a famous ball player, her bottom landing on the floor grid, scoring her like a waffle. Our mother scoops her up, and again she's wrapped in a blanket and again I take up a perch in the back seat on the way to the hospital. When the doctor is finished with her, she lifts her dress for me, and her bottom is covered with gauze. Now she has a bottom that looks like a waffle and a tooth that looks like a pirate's and no one can confuse us. Except I wish they could.

Chapter 11

In mid-August in Lowell, orange marigolds pop from postage-stamp yards often protected by stone Madonnas whose hands stretch over gardens of basil and peppers. I know this because in the mornings, before we go to the hospital, I run. I run past still-pajama'd toddlers who sleep no longer than I do, who sit on their front steps drinking milk from sippy cups or licking the jelly off their toast. If I run long enough and hard enough, my fear will erode. I think nothing except that I am running into the new day as if it is a shadow ahead, and if I begin by running, perhaps I can decide to live. Or perhaps my footsteps can take me backward to August 13 when I can still save my sister. If I remember to get up and run, if I pound to the other end of town and back, perhaps I have not disappeared.

Dan runs with me. He tells me months later that he ran because he feared Deane's killer would see me, the face he wants to kill. Dan takes aside my father and the FBI agents who come to the hospital and tells them his worries. But this is the world I no longer know—of details and plans. What I know is routine and mechanical. Running is the piece of the day I know how to do. I run in a T-shirt and shorts, struck by how much colder the air is than Knoxville's. When we return to the motel room, the clock's hands have moved, a piece of the day gone. Running is the easy part.

At the hotel, we eat breakfast with my parents and Deane's friends Sarah and Gary. Sarah looks at me while I sip my coffee, avoiding the newspaper. She puts her hand on top of mine, "Maybe you should think of getting a job."

I have a Tennessee Arts Commission grant that will help fund some months of writing, but she knows from her own losses that sitting alone at a desk is not the right occupation for mending. Her husky empathy anchors me. She hands me and my mother each a picture of Deane in a frame covered with red cloth, white hearts.

"I'll be at home tomorrow with Emi," she says, referring to her one-year-old daughter. "I need a day."

A day with Emi splashing water in a sink or pulling herself up on a chair. Nothing changes that, Sarah explains to me months later when I think about having a baby. Sarah understands the daily, its grounding. I envy her insight, her sense of what may help her. At that moment, respite is a concept I no longer understand.

Later, after the hospital, we go back early to the hotel to rest. Dan suggests that we go swimming, and I discover I want to. I dive into the cold water, pull myself up to the surface, my face breaking through, and I dive down again, feeling nothing but how good the water feels on my face. No one else is in the pool but Dan and me, and for these moments I feel happy—and guilty. I could be anyone sliding summer off her face with a swim. I swim up and down, up and down. I pull myself out and lie down on a deck chair in the sun. Is pleasure on this day an obscenity? Would Deane think so?

Earlier that day in the hospital hallway, I watch a man flirt with a woman with fiery red hair, a longtime friend of Deane's. She laughs, elated and sexy, and twists half away to give this man a glance. She does not see that I am watching. At that moment, I hate her oblivion, her resort to life. How dare she, when down the hall Deane lies dying? But I too turn my face up into the sky and feel the sun surround me, notice the orange marigolds, the slim breeze that chills my skin. Despite it all, life is what I can't ignore.

Among Deane's friends, I imagine what they must feel, what I feel: that we have escaped this time, except Deane, already marked, heading into sorrow. That is the surprise of death, that it destroys backward as well as forward. The past shifts too. Even there, she is someone whose whole life is waiting for two bullets.

One summer in college, Deane worked as a camp counselor, befriending a little girl who would not speak. Deane began to spend time at the girl's home at the mother's request, and soon the little girl began to whisper to Deane at camp. By the summer's end, the girl was speaking, and Deane felt the joy of her accomplishment. But she also felt she could do so much more if she had training. After college, she contacted a medical school, told the recruiter she was thinking about becoming a doctor.

"Can I watch an operation?" she asked.

The sight made her woozy. "I couldn't do it," she said. Instead, she applied to graduate school at the Eliot Pearson School of Child Study at Tufts, telling the story of the little girl, explaining her need for training. Mid-year there, her professors urged her to get a Ph.D. in psychology. The University of Michigan accepted her in its doctoral program.

"*We're* good at math," she said to me one day as she was doing statistics. "We just needed a reason to do it."

She spent five years in Ann Arbor, taking classes and seeing patients, and another four in Boston, writing her dissertation while she also worked, the paper she handed over to a typist the hour before she was shot. During that time, she married and filed for divorce, moved from Boston to Ann Arbor and back again. The people she noticed were the ones who seemed unburdened, who had time for a stroll. She longed to deliver her thesis the way overdue women long for birth.

"All I want is to grow a garden," she said. Every day she drove to the Radcliffe research center, carrying her box of research with her in the trunk of her car. "I'm terrified that my car will be stolen," she laughed. I teased her that soon she would have a glass house by the sea.

After her death, I wrote the introduction to her thesis, her colleagues bound it, and at graduation I walked across the stage to get her robe, her hood, her Ph.D.

The nurse tells my parents that she needs Deane's bed in critical care for a new patient. My parents respond with anger: the spot in critical care is

Deane's spot, where she will get the best care. Where she has a chance. No one else can have Deane's spot. What could the nurse be thinking? What the nurse is thinking, although she doesn't say so, is that she must give the bed to someone who may live.

"This will be good," I say to my parents. "Deane will have a room to herself. It will be easier to see her."

They turn their faces to me, confused that I have solved this for them. This is not an announcement of their daughter's certain death, but our chance to see her more easily. Their bodies recede back into themselves like animals out of danger, relieved by what they don't yet have to face.

The nurses move Deane, and soon they tell us her heartbeat is weakening, that we should gather. We stand around her bed, hold hands, now a large circle: my parents, Jeff, Dan, myself; Deane's friends Sarah and Gary; Art, Deane's former husband; and Michael, the man Deane was in love with. We listen to the beep and watch the jagged lines on the monitor that mean her heart is still beating. But we see the numbers are falling. And then the line goes flat. The nurse comes in to check and finds the line has been jostled loose, a mistake. Deane has died, we've said goodbye, and now she lives again. We actually laugh, dispelling the hiss of tension, as if Deane is there and has relieved us, doubled our chances to say goodbye. But the mistake exhausts us, and we disperse, disoriented. Deane died and now she is back and all I want is to lie down somewhere.

Chapter 12

Deane and I come together like a set, and other people don't. This earns us a lot of attention, and we don't question it. We can be an act if they want. And sometimes we are: our father now works for Campbell Soup Company, whose icons are twins—red-headed, apple-cheeked, plump—just like us. Once people learn our father works there, they assume that Deane and I are the prototype. *Are you the Campbell Soup twins?* they ask. *Yes*, we answer. Sometimes we almost believe it. At Halloween, we dress as the Campbell Soup twins, our curly red hair under white chef's caps marked with a capital C, our plump tummies behind white bib aprons. Our long-suffering brother is tucked between us, smothering inside a huge cardboard cylinder plastered with a poster-size Campbell Soup label. The three of us march in the Halloween parade around and around the school parking lot. Deane and I walk on either side of the can, and our brother knocks from side to side, screaming that we have shifted his peephole, entombing him in cardboard darkness.

"I can't breathe," Jeff says. "I can't see. I'm going to batter your faces in when we get home."

Deane and I are both embarrassed and proud: unlike the other children, we don't need masks or makeup. We embody disguise and trickery, and we know it. Let our brother scream. He's locked in a can. We swirl him around like he is today's lunch soup and wave to the crowd.

Our brother is by turns our champion, the one who protects us from bullies on the playground, and our nemesis, who hogs the TV and lies, his feet straight out, like a pole on the sofa so that Deane and I have to sit on the floor. He too is fat and unhappy about it, longing to be a football player but eating chocolate chip cookies by the bagful, resting them on his stomach so we can't get any.

"Watch this," he will say, standing suddenly and starting up his yo-yo show. "Here's Walk-the-Dog," he says as the yo-yo spasms lean slightly ahead of him, like a Chihuahua on a leash. He closes the door to the den, slips the lock in place so we can't run past him. Deane and I are his perfect captive audience. We sit just outside yo-yo distance, begging for Around the World, Shoot the Moon, the yo-yo spinning past his ear in circles. He starts using our heads as targets—or pretends to until he comes up with his next maneuver.

He deals with us like the commander of a small but important army. He names himself head of household security, forcing Deane and me—and even our baby-sitters—to participate in fire and burglar drills by climbing out the den windows.

"Mrs. Althouse," he says to the elderly, plump baby-sitter with a purse full of M&Ms. "Do you hear that noise? I think someone is in the house."

Mrs. Althouse, who actually believes him, plants her plentiful bottom on the window ledge and tries to swing her legs over. She climbs back inside and stands on the ottoman, sticking one leg out the window like a hoisted flag. Our brother takes her elbow and helps her set one foot on the ground while she slides her bottom toward him, tipping into the boxwood.

"Run, girls, run," shouts our brother.

"Run, girls, run," shouts Mrs. Althouse.

We lope across the yard to the house next door. The neighbor, Mr. Griffin, looks skeptical. But he returns with Jeff and a flashlight to look through the house. We watch from the Griffins' side door as the lights go on and off, upstairs and downstairs. They find no robbers, and Deane and I walk back along the street with Mrs. Althouse, who, disheveled and unnerved, casts suspicious glances at our cherubic brother.

"And just what did you hear, Jeff?" she asks him, staring him down.

"Rattling," he says. "Mr. Griffith thinks it's a shutter loose."

"Hmmmmfh," says Mrs. A, more content now as she eases amply back onto the sofa. She reaches into her bag and hands us each small bags of M&Ms like tranquilizers, keeping one for herself. Deane and I quickly divide them by color, pretending they are other foods, the red roast beef, yellow cornpone. Our plate is full. By that time Mrs. Althouse's purse is empty, and she is asleep.

Tricks are at least more exciting than Jeff's prayer meetings, when he reads to us from the Bible during his minister phase. He's a Bible-thumping preacher reading aloud from the scriptures, the black Bible in one hand while he jabs toward us with the other, pacing, all theatre and gravity:

"The Lord is our shepherd," he says, and he means it. Deane and I think he is acting like a dope. We prefer his yo-yo show.

"God loves this," says our mother, a Southern Christian fundamentalist-turned-Episcopalian, her voice cracking on *God* like frozen peanut brittle. *God* makes her cry.

By day, Rev. Foltz sets off firecrackers in the backyard.

"You been setting off firecrackers, son?" asks a policeman who pulls up to our house, his body broad as our mother's boxwood.

"My sisters, sir."

Upstairs, Deane and I hate our brother, his big arms, and bully body. The Lower Merion Township clink awaits. But the policeman leaves.

"Fire drill," he shouts later, opening the front door and pushing us out into the cold.

"I need my coat," I say, scratching to get back in. He hits my hand with his removed belt.

We run until we think he can't see us, run back to the back door and there he is, grinning through the glass panes, the door locked until Mom comes in.

"Mommeee," we greet her. "Make Jeff stop."

Jeff is our commander, but he is also fun. He lets us sit on top of his raised knees, surprising us with their collapse. We beg him for this game, and he acquiesces, lying on his back, his legs bent like tents. Or he lifts his feet, soles to the ceiling. Deane lies across them, her face hovering over his, her hands in his hands while he raises his feet like hydraulic lifts until she is flying over his body. He swings her back and forth, as if she is a small airplane that he operates. She crashes when he lets his legs lean to one side. And then it is my turn to fly over the geography of his face.

If our brother lost our mother's complete attention, he has ours. We love him for his powers of protection, his ability to produce bubble gum at any moment, his command of comic books. He is our first entrepreneur, urging his buddies to make cars or tree houses, bows or fishing rods. He is our general, leading us into whatever battle he invents: a fight for more Dr Pepper (then unavailable in the North), for better bedtimes, for louder fireworks.

He is also a mystery. Because of his elder status, we are certain that he knows what's up and we do not. His wavering between beneficence and malevolence seems entirely normal and justified by the mystery he has unraveled. The mood swings keep us on edge. Yes, he can ride us on his knees, but he can also steal our seats in the den or lock us out of our room or thump us on the back with his fist.

So we are afraid of him. But we also respect his straight-lipped perseverance. He sits at his desk, the crooked-neck lamp hanging over the paper he writes about forgiveness. *To err is human, to forgive divine,* the quote he's required to start with. Outside it grows dark, and still he sits staring down at his paper. Even at age eleven he has something to say. He has the air of a soldier slogging through boot camp, his seriousness cut by sadness.

"Help me with dinner, girls," Mom says. We hoist our bottoms up on the Formica counter, watch while she pulls out a bowl she fills with cornmeal, Crisco, and boiling water for cornpone.

Mom mostly makes cornpone—a baked version of salty, fried mush—when our dad isn't coming home. Jeff lies on his side on the couch, eating piece after piece, dipping them in ketchup, taking the last piece we want, and telling us to turn the channel to stupid shows like *Have Gun, Will Travel.* We don't know our brother or what makes him

unhappy. We think he's real smart but tortured by homework. Our dad
is never happy with him. He tells him he's too fat, that he needs to make
better grades, stay off the phone. Otherwise, our dad is too tired to notice much about any of us. He comes home at seven and fixes a drink, sits
to watch the news in the seat that Jeff owned minutes before.

"Hushhhhh," Dad says, baring his teeth, snapping at us all, if we are
not quiet while Walter Cronkite fills him in.

"Dad, I got an A on that forgiveness paper," Jeff says. Dad nods but
keeps staring at the TV.

"That's good," he murmurs. "I want to hear about it but not while I
watch the news, okay? Deane, is dinner almost ready? I'm huungery."
He twists the word around so that his hunger seems threatening—and
it is.

Jeff sits back down on the floor with us, quiet, his chin in his hands.
He doesn't turn to Dad again, just takes his plate in the kitchen and goes
upstairs. We hear his door close.

On weekends, Jeff hunts with our father, his friend skinny Ippy, and
Ippy's father. Ippy's dad owns Campbell Soup Company. The four of
them dress like fields of wheat brightened by red vests and crisscross
grassy acres flushing pheasants into the sky. At night they come home
with four or five birds tied together at the neck like onion bulbs. On
those days, Jeff's face is red with excitement.

"We got 'em," he says, dangling the corpses in front of our bewildered mother, who suspects these will go into her freezer. (They do. *Forever.*) But my father has moved on. He has turned on the news or opened
the newspaper. He has poured himself a drink. He has gone up to
shower. He has eased back into his shadowland of preoccupation. He is
thinking about what Ippy's dad said about Monday's meeting. He is
thinking about next week's trip to Italy, where the manufacturing plant
is not sterilized and twice as big as the company needs. He is not thinking about Jeff's happy face.

For a long time, Jeff thinks Dad will eventually shake free of his preoccupation and notice him. So he makes himself plain. He gets nineties
in French. He writes papers quoting the Bible. He starves himself to

make football weight. And then he gives up, lying on the couch with more chocolate chip cookies.

In school, Deane and I are called *Twinny, Twin, D and D, Foltzie.* We have one name like one person. We don't hate it, although we know that the person who calls us one name doesn't know which of us she's talking to. One woman who never calls us anything but *Twinny* has white, shiny teeth and scarlet lipstick that sometimes meanders beyond her lips. She smiles when she says *Twinny,* but the smile is not kind or warm. It expresses the discomfort she feels at our indistinguishable faces. We irritate her, the uncertainty we stir, the unease of never really knowing *Deane* or *Dorothy.* We don't trust her. We are learning what every twin learns: people who don't know our names are not paying attention. They are not mean or vindictive. They are lazy or indifferent. But we have names, and we prefer the people who use them.

We may be the only twins in our school, but we are old news. Our classmates don't try to make friends with just one of us. They want the twin pack. The fact of identity is blurred, the one sure blueprint unreliable. Two humans who look exactly alike make people laugh, make even us laugh. *Do you know which one you are? Do you ever switch places? Can you tell yourselves apart? Can your parents?*

We learn to use confusion, the one sure fact of our lives. In the summer, we go to the swimming pool every day. Deane and I love to swim. But our swimming teacher is spoiling for us to join the swim team. His enthusiasm transfers to our mother.

"Diana races," she says of a dark, skinny beauty younger than we are. We hate Diana and the idea of bashing our heads against the concrete walls, of flailing under the blows of muscled swimmers, of dying a suffocating death in splashing water. But shame pins us, Diana pins us, our mother pins us. Soon I am lined up in the row of swimmers, my toes gripping the edge. I stare into the lights that eclipse even my mother. I ready for the dive and as soon as I'm airborne I think, *I can't turn back.* I splat and my breath sinks, and the swimmer next to me sends splashing swats to drown me. But my arms keep churning, my lungs bigger than King Kong—and I win.

I am horrified.

Winning means I have qualified for the evening's finals. I will have to race again. But I'm not doing it twice. I wrap myself in a towel, and I beg Deane to go in my place, to pretend she is me. She nods, understanding her doom in advance, what's right about it. I watch her readying for a racing dive, and I love the deception. She dives in and when the race is over, she doesn't win. But we do: no one knows what we have done.

This scenario repeats itself whenever we want. And sometimes when we don't want. We go to the doctor for shots. The nurse gives Deane a shot. She turns to get the second needle, my shot. And goes after Deane again. We go to a church fair. I climb on a pony and circle the field. As Deane steps up for her turn, the church lady sizes her up.

"Hey, you just took a ride," she says. "Back to the end of the line, missy."

For most people, the insides they know become the outsides they present, appearances the easy measure. But what if the person we see is not herself but someone else? How unsettling to find your husband is not; he just looks like him. Spooky enough to be the horror behind the 1958 classic *Invasion of the Body Snatchers*, in which one by one loved ones are replaced by "pod people" who look just like them.

Only—and this is the important part—a twin does not think she looks just like her twin. The sameness is the joined soul, the blurred line between. Shaped by all the errors people make, you sometimes cannot shake the feeling you are someone else. Except that doesn't matter: it's all right to be whatever part of Deane I think I am. That is, at least early on, a comfortable confusion. To be a twin means nothing happens alone. Or if it does happen alone, it does not count. I sit down next to Deane in the dark, and I do not know why she is crying. But until she stops, I am crying too.

Chapter 13

All of us—my parents, Jeff, Dan, Art, Michael, Sarah, and Gary—now share a surreal intimacy—the near death and revival of Deane all because of a loose cord on her breathing machine. It is hard enough to slip inside someone's family as the new husband or lover. Here the niceties are suspended but not the awkwardness: Art, unfailingly quiet and polite, takes off his glasses, lowers his head. If the floor opened, it would be appealing. Dan too remains quiet, looking for something to do—find my mother a chair, get my parents some water, anything that will take him out of this room where too much has been seen and felt. He squeezes past me, whispering that he'll be right back. For Michael the situation has to be nightmarish. Before this day, he likely anticipated what meeting Deane's twin would be like and thought about the laughter we might have shared meeting, say, at my parents' house. He might have felt immediate relief that we were not alike and simultaneous confusion that we were. He might have imagined meeting my parents, perhaps when his relationship with Deane was further along. Now he is intimate with our present, knowing that the intimacy has no future.

We go back to the hotel. A friend has sent a care box: a garbage bag of popcorn she has popped herself, a bottle of gin, a salami and cheese. What seems so irreverent of grief and its dried appetites is just right, a vividness. My parents, Dan, Michael, and I gather in our hotel room and pour ourselves drinks in plastic glasses, sitting in a circle around the popcorn that sits like a boxing bag in its center. Michael tells how he met Deane at a Cambridge mixer.

"We talked. And then she came back and said, 'Do you want to talk some more?'" She was beautiful and shy and direct. I couldn't believe my luck. 'Of course I want to talk some more.'"

Michael is German, blond and tall and soft-spoken. At the news of Deane's shooting, he flew back from Heidelberg, where he was spending the summer. He and Deane had met only that spring but already planned a life together, and for Deane the summer dragged without him.

"We drove to Martha's Vineyard," she says. "And we sang the whole way."

I am always angry at Deane when she picks men, always men I wouldn't choose, so that her choice seems secret, the one thing I'm not allowed. It's not that I don't like her husband. I do. But he is taboo and foreign in the way that sharing Deane is foreign. He doesn't get to have her. But I know he does. And although I am happy for her, I am filled with confusion. How far away will she go from me and how soon?

When she met Art, he was teaching history with his friend at a private high school in Cambridge, Massachusetts. They were at a party together, and the subject of nuns came up.

Art turned to my sister. "You would have made a beautiful nun," he said in a voice so low she could barely hear him.

"Oh. Thank you," she said, utterly charmed.

They began to see each other, and she spent time in his cold, spare apartment, where he introduced her to heaping dishes of brown rice and cheeses, sprouts, and granolas. He's tall and wiry, with brown eyes and lots of straight, brown hair, horn rims, a Harvard degree in Chinese history, a full laugh, and warm smile, a man more comfortable in L.L. Bean flannel than tie.

His mother was a Boston blueblood raised by maids on Beacon Hill, so sheltered that when she married she wrote out a recipe for serving her new husband corn flakes and milk. He was a lawyer who left the family early, when Art was a young boy, the last of three children, a sorrow he had never recovered from, his sadness palpable. But when they met, that wasn't Art's defining feature. I met him soon after he and Deane began dating and liked him, his exuberant embrace of me, the way he had of hugging me hello so that my feet left the floor and swung side to side.

"Doey," he'd say, his nickname for me.

They came to see me when I was living in Iowa City, in graduate school at the Writers' Workshop.

"I love him," Deane told me, the happiest I'd seen her.

When she got into graduate school at the University of Michigan, he went with her.

They set up a Spartan New England household that Hawthorne would have liked, the furniture covered in forest greens and deep maroons, not the feminine delicacy I associated with my sister, more woodcutter than cashmere. My unease started. And so did theirs. A man in Deane's Ph.D. program began to attend to her, come over to the house to spend time with both Deane and Art. Eventually, he told Deane he loved her and left his wife. His attention, his precipitous action unsettled Deane; she was glad when he left the program, and for a while she closed the door on whatever he had made her feel. Later she realized her unease was a warning, an undercurrent of indecision about Art.

I too fell in love with a quiet man who looked like he just marched out of a lumber camp: Dan Gray, the son of a Pittsburgh milkman and the second in the family to get a college degree (his sister, older by ten years, beat him by only three months). He was a bright kid in a town of football players and car nuts. He chose football, and his quarterback's arm got him a football scholarship to the University of Pennsylvania.

During his first months there he carried a pocket dictionary: he heard so many words he'd never heard in Penn Hills. He'd look the strange words up and realized he'd read them all. He'd just never heard anyone say them.

I take Danny to Ann Arbor to meet Deane and Art. That night, we go to the movies, and in the ladies' room Deane bursts into tears.

"You are doing it again," she says, referring to my penchant for falling in love too quickly. "Is he crazy too?" She cries as if I'd said I am moving to Australia, and I am furious that she thinks I am still choosing men no good for me.

"Danny is different," I say.

She hates not Danny but my blind passions, my love of immersing myself in something before I'd really thought about it. She isn't giving Danny a pass. Is she as sure that Dan would take me from her, as Art had taken her? But Danny and Art are remarkably complementary: both quiet, both intellectual, both bearded and thoughtful. They become friends, both privy to the strange sharing they have to do with twin sisters.

Now, at the hospital—a year and a half since Deane and Art separated, since we have seen Art—the two men share an unease. Deane and Art left Ann Arbor—Deane had only her thesis to finish, and Art had finished an art degree—and bought a house in Somerville that they soon realized they couldn't afford. Deane had her part-time job at Stoney Brook while she wrote her thesis, and Art set up an art studio. The house is beautiful but large and drafty, and its empty rooms are more portentous than welcoming. Danny and I visit Deane and Art in a cold June, and we go to see Art's studio. That is where Deane finds a cache of letters from the woman Art met in art school. He and Deane had gone out with her and her husband, had had them to dinner. Deane did not tell me about the affair for a long time, but one day I saw a lamp broken in their bedroom. "We had a fight," Deane said, "and I threw it."

She looks at me, her big eyes spilling with fury and grief. "He told me it was over. But she's still writing him. I'm walking home." I go with her, although Deane doesn't talk. It's clear how unhappy she is, how sad. I make sticky buns for a brunch at Deane's friend's home and discover too late that I have used salt instead of sugar.

That fall Deane calls me in mid-afternoon. "It gets dark so early here," she says. She's eating a fat meatball grinder she bought on the way home. "We're applying to be house parents at Tufts," she says. "We can't afford the house."

Deane found them the job. They interview together, and Deane doesn't want to answer the questions they ask about her and Art. But they get the job, and for a while it seems right. Until Deane calls me to say she's moving out. All this time she's kept it quiet, found an apartment with an old friend, found the dorm job so Art would not be strapped, kept her mouth shut to protect his privacy, to protect hers. I admire her, but I am hurt that she did not tell me.

"It was between Art and me," she said. "I had to pick Art."

I am surprised because I thought Deane and Art were just like Danny and me. Or maybe I am just too busy trying to right myself in my own relationship. Danny and I married while we were living in Chicago, and two months later we moved to Ann Arbor to be with Deane and Art, giving up decent jobs for no jobs. We are trying to get used to having to tell each other where we are going, a task I resent. We get part-time jobs—I a secretary, he a nighttime janitor—so we can both write part-time. But lousy jobs and no cash does not make a good marriage.

Danny and I are untangling our own nest of splits. Most of the time, Danny and I have an easy friendship. We teach English at the same community college outside Knoxville, Tennessee, where we moved from Ann Arbor after we found teaching jobs there. During the day, we pass each other between classes, too busy to stop for lunch or even office visits. At home after school, we jog past arts and crafts bungalows and Victorian gingerbreads on jutting sidewalk stones to the mostly abandoned road that ran past the Emory River, talking about the day's gauntlet of stresses as we run. At night we cook together in our big, peeling kitchen, drinking wine as we roast spaghetti squash full of cheese or peel garlic for pasta.

But I hate Tennessee and leave my teaching job three months before Deane's death, a move that Danny feels is a kind of abandonment, an unexpected shift in the parallel lives we planned. He does not support the move, but I make it anyway, which leaves me feeling both shaky and frightened. I leave, I say, to write, to find a writing-related job. I want to leave Tennessee, but Danny says he doesn't believe a move will change my unhappiness; he wants me to try therapy first. I find a therapist who tells me I see my world peopled with critical fathers. I talk about wanting a baby.

I talk and push and cry with Danny about wanting one. "I already raised a child," he says, meaning his sister, ten years younger than himself. "I don't want children, not yet."

My life is stuck, and it is Danny's fault. I am living in a town so small the postman knows I am a writer, and people on the street know that I am a runner. In 1981, women in Harriman, Tennessee—population about five thousand—don't run the streets in shorts. Every morning, at the town's restaurant, at one round table sits the mayor, the school superintendent, the bank president, and the police chief, and sometimes a stray school board member. And everyone else mopping their biscuits and gravy and fried chicken livers knows not to sit there. I feel I've been dropped by a parachute. I can't buy the New York Times or even buy a bottle of wine in a city founded in 1889 by Temperance Movement activists. The deed on our house forbids drinking within its walls, an ordinance we ignore. I love Danny, but my real life, the one I'd been headed for in graduate schools in big cities—New York, Chicago, Boston—has somehow disappeared. I am teaching community college students who either don't speak or fall asleep, and I see no way out. We have bought a turn-of- the-twentieth-century Victorian house for $30,000 that siphons off our money. Tree roots grow in the plumbing, and paint and muscle are all we can afford. I am mad at Dan for loving Appalachia, for getting me to sign on, for not having children, for not making money. Is this my real life?

Danny is so quiet, and I learn his quiet has facets—the smoldering rocking one, the set-chin one, the eyes-closed one. He is as angry at me and my discontent as I am at him. We are still friends, we love each other, but our fights are sculpting themselves, the ones that are ours, the same set, over and over. And fights scare Danny: his family didn't have them, not out loud or at least directly. Fighting is what I did with Deane: I knew we could fight, and fights would evaporate fast. What I don't know is what transfers to a marriage. A twin's intimacy is not replicated, although that's all I want or recognize. And wanting that is too much for Danny, too unfair, disrespectful. I fell in love with him for his boundaries. He knows who he is apart from me. But I am mad at him because he is also not a part of me as Deane was. His is a separateness I'd not met before, or at least not one I want.

We go back to the hospital, and for a while, I sit next to Deane, holding her hand while the breathing machine sighs in and out. Here we are. Two sisters who want from their husbands, from everyone, what they have only in each other: an understanding and merger that, perilously consuming, is also what we understand as love.

Chapter 14

Our life is full of comparisons. Deane is smarter. Deane is prettier. Deane is more popular. Deane gets her homework done faster. I like you better than Deane. You talk more than Deane. You laugh more than Deane. You are the subject of other people's hard work, their efforts to stop the riddle. But their riddle is different from the riddle you face: Is there a difference? Or are we the same? Can I be a separate person? Will anyone ever like me just because I am Dorothy? The questions that every person faces in forging an identity are larger. You do not know who you are—or who you are not.

What separates twins from singletons may be trust, the kind of shrugging trust you give to your own mutterings, to your dirty skin at the end of the day, to your body in the shower, to the sheets that help you sleep. There are no feelings you feel for your twin that you do not feel for yourself. It is no bother, the communion back and forth, no held breath, no second guess. *What will she think of me* is a question twins do not have about each other. *What will she do without me* is the question.

We are at an elementary school in the Italian section of Philadelphia where we're bused every day while builders finish our school in Gladwyne. We have a separate classroom, separate recess, separate lunchtimes. It's as if there are no other children in the school but us. Except we see them outside the windows during their recess, and we meet on the sidewalk during fire drill. In the lunchroom, we eat apart but we eat the same food:

wax beans and fat spaghetti soft as the white of a fried egg. I push my tray away, and one of *their* teachers walks over.

"You can't go outside until you finish."

The food is unfriendly, bitter, mean like a bad boy with jagged teeth. I cry through the beans and the squirmy noodles. I learn what's hard to put in my mouth.

A lesson I don't know. Deane and I have grown round on our mother's Southern cooking—cornpone and fried chicken, buttered doughnuts and caramel cake. At recess, we buy penny candy and my leftovers spill onto the classroom floor as I hang up my coat on the row of classroom hooks.

"Don't buy so much," Mrs. Baker, our second grade teacher says, standing over me.

While I clean up my mess, the whole class staring, I look at Deane, her face my shield. She shakes a Kodak canister at me, a small orange tin two inches tall we fill with cinnamon hearts instead of film, easy to sneak when the teacher isn't looking.

"TTS," she mouths.

Two-Ton Sisters. Our bathtub nickname. We have what the world says are the wrong bodies, fat ones. Except our bodies are identical. In the bath, we count the rings of flesh our bellies make, one, two, three. How can my body be wrong if Deane's is just like it? We watch a *Twilight Zone* episode in which a grotesquely deformed human is sent into space by his grieving parents. When he lands on some new planet, all the creatures look just like him. In fact, he's the handsomest of them all.

Sharing features in American culture, perhaps any culture, is a good thing. *You look like my cousin, my favorite aunt, my third-grade teacher.* People want to look like someone else, not themselves alone. From the time a baby is born, we search his face for distant features he has borrowed. Two generations back you find his nose or missing tooth or twisted finger, and start to smile. *Guess whose nose he has.* Deane and I don't have to go so far. We are each other's new planet, and there we look fine.

Still, fat children's bodies seem all wrong to them, partly because their friends are so small, with legs thin as forearms, and forearms like candles.

Our mother loves clothes, dresses with waists, skirts with pleats, plaids that lose their pattern over our bellies. Her passion is our torture: finding clothes that are big, childish, and identical is tough work. So our mother makes one exception: we are allowed to buy one version in separate colors, blue and red. Otherwise our clothes are exactly alike. Our mother sometimes even buys a version for herself, the mother-daughter '50s fashion. But locked in a dressing room, our mother is less than delighted.

"I can take up the hem," she says, running her hand inside our skirt waistbands. To fit our waists, wide as car tires, we wear dresses cut for children far taller than we are. The skirts hang to the floor.

When regular-size clothes stop fitting us, our mother takes us to Lane Bryant, a store for fat people. Deane and I lie on the car floor so none of our friends will see. In the parking lot we duck our heads into our jacket hoods, run inside the store, weave past the svelte mannequins. Deane and I look behind them: bunches of fabric clump at their backs, held together by clothespins. On our way to the dressing rooms, we see girls bigger, older, fatter than we are. We go home and sit on the hill below our dining room window. We decide to run in circles until our fat melts off. Until our mother calls us in to dinner. Until we get hungry.

The form we are in seems inescapable. It is simply our shape in the world, and we are unlucky. Our mother tells us we should eat less, and sometimes she puts us on diets she rips out of magazines. Toast without butter. Chicken breasts without skin. Pasta without sauce. We hide saltines in the den, and when she's not there, we pull them out, nibbling the squares into guns.

At school, Mr. D. B., the gym teacher, hates fat kids. He lets us sit on the sidelines like lumps. We are picked last for teams. When I strike out, I want to slide under home base. But mostly I want to make Mr. D. B. fat and pick him last. Fat makes us sad in the world but not between each other. It doesn't keep us inside the house on a sofa either. We run through the yard pretending we are horses, or swim under water, porpoises. We climb trees; we sled and skate. Deane and I have something the other D. B.'d fat children don't have: each other.

Chapter 15

Each morning all of us meet in the hotel dining room for breakfast, the newspaper headlines a danger we skirt past on our way to a table. We could be a wedding party or a family reunion, only we're not. We bow our heads to our food—an English muffin, a broken egg. We drive to the hospital, enter its mist of antibiotic soap. This morning I walk into Deane's room and put my arms around her. When I do, the nurse sitting by the window begins to cry. Jeff has placed a piece of red carpet blessed by the Pope in Deane's hand. I never ask how we got such carpet, but I like its suggestion of power. If medicine can't bring my sister back, magic may: the Pope, the vaulted sky, the radio waves.

Jeff has been again the brother I remember from the playground, shielding me from bullies. In this case, he runs social interference, letting me lie down alone in a hospital room while he talks to roomfuls of visitors. When he sees how annoyed I am by my mother's hovering, her insistence on following me when I visit Deane first in the intensive care unit, then in her room, he pulls me back, her back with a word.

"Not now," he says, enough to make us slink into our chairs.

I am ashamed of pettiness, of not wanting my mother with me. He is lovely to her. Yet he makes a mistake as he speaks by phone to a colleague.

"There is no hope," he says, just as my mother walks in. He quickly hangs up.

"There's always hope," she says, a plea for reassurance.

"Of course there is," he says.

He is pained by my father's negotiations, his efforts to find the best neurosurgeon, to somehow corporately organize Deane out of death. Jeff shields himself from those details, walks away from Dad's phone calls. Instead, he comes and sits next to me.

"How you doing?" he asks, not expecting anything. He puts his arm around my shoulder and leaves it there, a gate of protection.

A friend of Deane's comes up. Jeff stands up to greet her.

"She was so quiet, and then she'd say just the right thing," the woman says, her eyes filling with tears. "Are you getting any rest?"

"She did do that," my brother says, shaking his head, looking at me. He smiles at the woman. "How did you know her?"

"We met years ago, in a women's group," she says. "How are your parents?"

My brother looks over at them. "In shock. We all are. Thanks for coming over." He takes my elbow and I sit down again, too tired to speak, to draw out of myself what speaking to strangers requires. But he keeps standing, talking as long as she wants, even bantering, smiling. He is so good at it, at shielding me from what I cannot do.

Later that day, Dan and I drive to Deane's apartment in Medford. It's in the sixties, and I've brought only gauzy Tennessee clothes, so I go to get warmer ones from Deane's closet. Her roommate Lynn lets us in, and I climb the stairs to Deane's room, where her open suitcase lies on the bed. I take a sweater we bought together from her closet—one I also have in Tennessee. On the hour's drive back to the hospital, I fall asleep and dream about her. Standing, she smiles and falls back in a chair, her head bandaged, her face joyous as if she'd come to release me from sorrow, to reassure me that she is all right.

Each day is the same: a routine of visiting Deane, seeing her friends, making phone calls, ordering food we don't eat, returning to the hotel. Soon the doctor asks us to consider how long we want Deane on a respirator. He tells us her body will not live long, even with that help. We put off the decision, certain we won't have to make it and afraid that we will.

On the eighth day, before we leave the hospital, the nurse rubs Vasoline on the drying skin around Deane's eyes, and Deane begins to heave, her body rejecting the respirator. When I open her eyelids and look into her blue eyes, she does not look back. Wherever she is going she has already gone. She is already the dream in my head.

A nurse calls at 2 a.m. Saturday morning, August 22, and tells us to hurry. Dan and I dress in the dark cold and join my parents, so somber and still. When we arrive at the hospital, the nurse tells us Deane died at 2:04. Dad, Mom, Jeff, and I enter her room. The nurse has already removed the respirator, and Deane looks more like herself than she has all week, her chest its normal size, her face soft. I put my arms around her, without lines and the respirator in the way, and I kiss her. A nurse comes in behind me and stands, watching. After a moment she says, "What you are doing is unhealthy."

I look up at her, unable to take in what she is saying.

"It isn't healthy," she says again. "It isn't sanitary."

"Can you leave us for a minute, please," my father asks.

As she turns to go, my brother follows her. "What in the hell is wrong with you?" he asks. "Damn you."

Chapter 16

The Commonwealth of Massachusetts

To: The Sheriffs of several counties or their Deputies, the State Police, the Constables and Police Officers of any City or Town in said Commonwealth, or to any or either of them,

We command you that immediately, without delay, you take the body of James Palmer (if he may be found in your precinct) and him safely keep, so that you forthwith have him before our Justices of our Superior Court, now holden at Cambridge within and for said County of Middlesex, then and there in our said Court to answer us upon an indictment against him for Murder.

September 1, 1981

Chapter 17

Every Wednesday Deane and I head to the cold basement of St. Christopher's Episcopal Church and sing to Oscar Eiermann. We have joined the choir because the Brownie Scout Troop has no more room, and we are heartbroken. Oscar is formidable, a big man with a wide face, greased hair, and a mole on his cheek. He makes us try out by singing solo. One by one, he calls us to the piano, and we warble any tune he chooses. At home I am a diva, pulling my dress sleeve off my shoulder, belting out lyrics in a quivery voice I dig for. In front of Oscar, my lips barely open. The home opera star is dead to me. But "dead" is apparently the one spot in the choir Oscar hasn't filled. I am granted a place, and Deane is too.

The choir dresses are floor-length red robes covered by white smocks. Only they have no more robes our plump size. So Deane and I wear gathered, red-felt Christmas skirts that stop above our knees. On Sunday, because we are the shortest, we lead the choir members into the sanctuary, and as we walk down the aisle we hear laughter. But we are glad to belong nevertheless. We enter singing behind the minister and acolyte carrying the huge, gold cross. This must be theatre, I think. I love the eyes on me, the solemn bow to the cross, the beautiful songs. I love coming to the church at night for practice, singing to the black windows, the empty pews, the lit altar. To be where no one else is allowed, the choir's special dispensation. We walk into the mysteries. We are the pilgrim families singing, the gusts outside and far away. The stone floor takes our footsteps, echoes our notes. We lift our voices, and Oscar holds them high with the tilt of his raised hand, the languid middle finger, the sudden jab into the blank church air.

Oscar is ambitious, and he has another life. He conducts the Gilbert and Sullivan productions in Philadelphia, and he invites our choir to a performance. We dress in velvet and sit in the balcony and watch *Pirates of Penzance*. We yawn and fall asleep in the heated dark, but we also stare at Oscar, fascinated by his place in a foreign world, the way he directs grown men and women with the same fingers, the same waves and thrusts. These women are not our mothers: their busts lift into the air as if connected to the roof by wire. Their faces turn to the lights and out of their throats float trills we realize they also auditioned for. *Every moment brings a treasure/of its own especial pleasure./ Though the moments quickly die,/Greet them gaily as they fly*. . . . They skip to the right and left, bouncing on slippered feet, and we can't imagine the lives that brought them there.

Oscar *knows* Philadelphia, he *knows* actors, he *knows* theatre, and even so he comes twice a week to Gladwyne to direct rich, voiceless, Episcopalian girls. His ambitions extend to us. He enters us in a choir contest in a huge Philadelphia cathedral. Choirs from all over the city fill the pews in purple or gold or scarlet robes like ours. But we are tiny in the vault of the church sky. And the empty air that floats over our heads makes us believe in two heavens—this church one and the thick invisible notes of the inexplicable. All day, one by one, the choirs get up to sing. When it is our turn, we climb onto bleachers in front of enormous gold organ pipes, Deane and I side by side at the choir's heart. Oscar's face is softened by expectation. We are all so scared we know we will sing like rusty gates. The cross will darken, and God will press the bad notes back through our teeth, and we will die from crammed heads. But then Oscar pulls notes out of our mouths hand over hand like a woman hauling hanging laundry back toward her open window. Our voices become prayers of music, spreading out into the still church, over the flagstones and the prayer books and the communion plates. We sing "The Prayer from Hansel and Gretel," and it is the right song for children, a sweetness of belief that only someone under twelve could sing.

> *When at night I go to sleep,*
> *Fourteen angels watch do keep.*
> *Two my head are guarding:*

Two my feet are guiding:
Two are on my right hand;
Two are on my left hand;
Two who warmly cover;
Two who o'er me hover;
Two to whom 'tis given
To guide my steps to Heaven.

And the thing is, we win. We win the whole thing. We beat out every choir in Philadelphia, and we win money. The next week on the pulpit the minister smooths a white pulpit cloth embroidered in blue and gold and green. The cloth our voices won. Deane and I wear long robes after that.

The church is huge in our life—like a big stone conscience away from home, a place to read about Chinese children who aren't allowed to do anything but study, or children like Jesus who had to ride around on burros, or the American Indian children we imagine once lived in our backyard. We are born just past danger, it seems, and church is the place to think this out and maybe feel a little gratitude if there is enough room after all the guilt and boredom.

For a time, Thursdays are family night at the rectory, and all the mothers bring the same casseroles—chicken tetrazzini or tuna noodle casseroles or beef stew we scout through until we find our mother's. Afterward, a grown-up shows a movie about people in other countries who need help. We sit eating our slices of apple pie—there are boxes and boxes of apple pie—sneaking back for another slice and another. Until we can't bear the heated dark, and we creep into the empty hallways, down the stairs into our Sunday school classrooms, and finally out into the cold sky whose stars only make the air seem colder. In the dark, we pretend we are inside a Hardy Boys book, and at any noise we scream, certain ghosts rise from the cemetery, coming if not for us, then for our stolen pie. In the dark, everyone looks alike. That is, no one has looks at all. No one is fat, and no one is a twin. It is easy to feel lucky.

Chapter 18

My sister dies, and then she disappears. My parents, brother, Dan, and I descend in the hospital elevator, blinking as it closes doors until we hit the basement, where, though none of us says so, we know Deane must be. We do not ask. We go down the windowless halls among the odors of antiseptic death until we step outside again breathing cool Massachusetts air.

At the hotel, we pack and gather for breakfast. Then the newspapers arrive. In the paper where the shootings corner the headlines are stories of Reagan and Israel, of OPEC, of Willie Nelson and Barbra Streisand, cigarette ads, and ads for greyhound racing. The weather headline: sunny. Then I spot the blunt header that must be news of someone else: shooting victim dies. The bald, public summary of a news event in Lowell, Massachusetts. An American story of workplace death. Of one thousand people murdered at work each year, an average of twenty homicides a week.

On another morning about another family, we too might be reading. We too would wonder what another family is feeling. But now we are *that* family, and it seems to us that the news is not about Deane but something else no longer our story. Our story this minute is much smaller. In the corner of the restaurant, we see the family of Barbara Kaplan, Deane's colleague wounded in the shooting. My father, mother, and I stop at the table, and Barbara's mother's eyes fill with tears as she tells us Barbara has lost an eye. "I'd settle for an eye," my father says.

Two policemen come to the hotel to see my father—a fact I learn many years later and never from him—to report what the doctors found: a wound just above and behind Deane's right ear, another through her neck, the bullet fragments in her brain.

We climb into the car and ride to the airport. I stare out the window at Lowell, its shut factories. Deane had once pointed out the empty buildings and talked about how the world had moved on, leaving Lowell a hardscrabble place. Did Lowell's despair become her killer's, become his family's, his father a police chief with too much to enforce? Her killer, a man raised where the landscape is failure. No one speaks. We ride in exhausted air.

At the airport, we board before other passengers and sit in privacy. I wonder if Deane's coffin is below us, her autopsied body where men are loading cargo.

"Is she here?" I ask my father.

"She is," he nods, taking my hand. "She's here."

Strangers understand the rules about death better than I do, the plans made for lifting Deane to Philadelphia. My sister sits somewhere, but I have no idea where. I want to fly with her, but I never bring up the wish. My father had arranged the details with the hospital, death a protocol placed on paper. That morning, far down the hospital hall, leaning on the nurses' counter, he signed sheet after sheet. I had not known how many secrets death held, how much privacy, how much unseen, unsaid. Or how practical it is; like anything else, death insists on organization. The time for an autopsy, the place, the doctor, and police witnesses. What were they looking for?

"She wasn't a soldier," my father says, his voice jagged, cracking. "She wasn't in a war."

We are sitting in first class, the only time I have flown that way, its wide leather seats, its illusion of privacy.

"Deanie, do you want something to drink?" my father asks my mother. He orders them each a scotch, Diet Cokes for Dan and me.

My mother has moved into another stage. At the hospital, she moaned, a long low sound, when she saw Deane. She walked to her, put her purse down, leaned over, and put her hand on her forehead as she always did when we were sick, to take our heat's measure. The tears rolled down her cheeks silently, and she bent to kiss my sister. But now something inside has stilled or scurried back where she won't have to look. She talks about anything but the one thing, like someone afraid, and she is. My dad helps her into the car, packs her night bag into the back.

"Did you call Po?" my dad asks, referring to my mother's sister.

"She and Ginger will meet us," says my mom.

I too am in shock, and it is something I have not felt before, the forms it takes, its denial and bravado. Life in shock is easy, like being drunk. The air looks like air, and you think you are calm. But you are behind a curtain, like illness. You reside far away, a person from the wrong end of binoculars. Another person slots into your place, more perfect than you are. She makes phone calls, talks to reporters, throws parties, makes grief comfortable, reassures everyone that you, locked inside, are fine. You depend on a person you have never met before.

My mother's shock is like that but different. She is perfect but she is also drinking.

"Do you have anything to wear to the funeral?" she turns to ask me. "Warren says he'll come whenever we want him," she says, mentioning the minister. "I'm thinking the service on Wednesday," she says to my father, taking another drink from the stewardess. "In the afternoon. With white flowers and 'Onward Christian Soldiers,'" she says, naming her favorite hymn.

And then she starts to cry again, her chin dipping into her chest, her tears in her drink.

"Deane, stop, please don't," my father says, his own tears sliding down his face, both of them retreating into the roar of the plane's engines. I look out the window, the first of my looking everywhere for Deane, as if the clouds could part and pass her to me.

When we deplane in Philadelphia, my mother, too bright, too loud, offers Deane's Michael to my unmarried cousin, Ginger, who greets us.

"He's really cute," my mother says, veering down an alley of the inexplicable.

"Mother," I scream at her, furious, amazed, ashamed of her stupid insensitivity. He was her new love, the start of a new life. I can't help but think how angry Deane would be—and to Ginger, whom to us represented beauty and success, the New York model whom every man would want. Ginger has the grace to be as embarrassed as I am. She puts her head down and laughs uncomfortably, puts her arm around my shoulder. My beautiful Aunt Po with her soft smile puts her arms around my mother.

"Come on, Deanie. How was the flight? We'll get your bags."

She and Dad flank my mother, who is drunk, who is somewhere I recognize from childhood, the times when she couldn't address emotion. Yet, sometimes she was the world's comfort.

"Those kids are mean to you because they're jealous," she'd say to my fat, teased, third-grade self, and for that moment all my worries disappeared. But other times, that woman was gone and someone meaner stepped up.

"Your petootie is sticking out," she told Deane once, meaning her pubic bone.

She was far more fragile than we understood as children. We just knew sometimes we didn't have access; it was as if the soft, sweet mother had turned to salt.

"You need a little girdle," she told Deane.

Aunt Po takes one of my mother's arms, Ginger the other, and they walk her down the airport hall. I walk beside them, but I am not talking. I don't want to make this easy for anyone. Although I am supposed to: it's my new job to take away awkwardness and fear, to help people understand they don't have to take care of me. When I am acting as Deane or on Deane's behalf, I know what to say. I want her to be proud of me, of the way I care for the people she loved. Otherwise, I want to draw the curtains, slip out of my body, move into empty-headedness like a new apartment.

Chapter 19

We reach my parents' house. A palm-green brick two-story built in the 1930s, it anchors the bottom of a slope surrounded by stone walkways, ivy, pines, and a single magnolia. The slope continues past the house, the end of its decline marked by four beds of peonies, followed by a flat field, and bordered by forest. The yard is a series of moving pictures of Deane and me. I stare out the window, and there we are.

All day the phone rings, the doorbell rings. My brother and I are exhausted from fixing drinks and food, but grateful for something to do; we are operating a bar and grill. We open the door to my parents' friends, who rush in with casseroles and pots of soup. When we greet one wide-eyed, stricken couple whom we don't recognize, my brother turns to me, "Stephen's parents?"

Stephen is an old friend of mine who showed up at the hotel in Lowell, a similar look on his face, so frantic we had to calm him. A friend says to me that in disaster every caller wants something, and she is right: a job, an assurance, a role, a reprieve from the fear of you. Who will you be, after all? You must help some speak, some relax, some not be loco. A local reporter calls, and I agree to talk to her because I know I will get it right. One article turns us into twin freaks; we eat in lockstep, we pee in lockstep, we sleep in lockstep. Another says Deane liked pretty things.

This is my first death, and I am ignorant of the details that keep each mourner too busy and tired to be alone with fear and grief. Warren, the minister, comes, and we sit in the living room to choose music and prayers, pallbearers, and flowers. He brings prayer books and passes them to us, asks us to turn to the "Burial of the Dead." He begins with a prayer, our heads down.

"Do you want a viewing?"

"Yes," I say. "But private, not everyone."

"We can do that in the morning, a separate time several hours before the funeral." My mother is nodding yes.

"I want Sarah to come," I say, including Deane's best friend. My parents again nod yes.

"Do you want communion?" Warren asks. My parents look at me. I shake my head.

"It's too long," says my father.

"There are a number of psalms," Warren says. We scan them and I ask for the 23rd psalm, a psalm I connect with Deane and grade school and saying it over and over as a child without any idea of what it meant. Warren reads it now, and I hear it for the first time. Perhaps we all do. *He maketh me to lie down in green pastures. . . . Yea, though I walk through the valley of the shadow of death, I will fear no evil.*

"And the music?"

I ask for Bach, a cantata. In college Deane took music, but she was no good at it, at knowing which composer wrote what. One morning, facing a music exam, she played Bach for me and began to dance, her hand to her hip and in the air again, Travolta disco embedded in Bach's elegance.

The church would play that.

Warren takes us through "The Burial of the Dead." I scour the words for some clue about what Deane faces, about where she's gone.

"Accept our prayers on behalf of thy servant Deane, and grant her an entrance into the land of light and joy."

I want in every word the clasp of the nun's hand again: *Your sister is in Paradise.* Warren tells when we will enter, stand, and sit. He carves us a path, ends the work with a prayer, and my sister-in-law begins to cry.

We go to the funeral home, a Victorian house converted for the dead. My mother and I meet with the cosmetologist who will prepare Deane for a family viewing. He works in something like the back of a flower shop, cool with glass cases and metal tables.

I have brought Deane's rose dress and gold hoops with me. I look down on her face, and it is not Deane I see, but some wax version. Without life, no one's face can be what it was. We are not our looks at all, but the energy that lights our features. So this is her body, not Deane. Already she seems far away. Ten days ago she was coming to visit, and I stood in my yard gathering apples. Now I deliberate the choices of a clothed afterlife.

My sister lies on the table like a patient, and I remember a D. H. Lawrence short story: neighbors carry a dead miner into an English cottage where his wife bathes his body and dresses him for burial, pushing away her fear, moving by rote, feeling how set apart death places them.

"Was this what it all meant—utter, intact separateness, obscured by heat of living?" asks the miner's wife.

I am here for my sister, but I also shut down my belief in normality, in the daily, in the ease of one breath after another. My mother is calm and distant; an outsider might say disinterested. But I know she is not even here. She talks with me about the details—makeup, hair—but she lets me make the decisions. I realize how small my mother is, her thin, rounded shoulders, her fine bones. I see her and what has brought us here before this man who picks over my sister. And I know too that she and I will never again talk about this moment.

Chapter 20

Our mother doesn't think of us as oddities so much as double her luck. She never confuses us or treats us as one person. That she knows who I am, distinct from Deane, makes me feel solid. I am not just wristband A or B. She knows I am fiery, and Deane her sweet child. She never calls me Deane, the only person except Deane and my brother to get my name straight, 100 percent.

Our father loves to mix us up, especially in front of colleagues. He bends down to me, turns to his friend, "This is Deane."

I laugh. Perfectly. He laughs too, embarrassed, smiling at his buddy, as if to say, *Look at this phenomenon. I'm the father, and I can't even tell.* It is, we eventually realize, a form of bragging. He knows who we are, but he likes the circus stir we create. As we get older, his pretense is alarming. If he doesn't know who we are, what can he love about each of us? We want him to be certain, as we are not. I want him to know who I alone can become. If we are only interesting when we are indistinguishable, maybe distinction is dangerous. *DeaneDorothy DeaneDorothy.* Dad stands at the top of the stairs, calling out the profusion of our inseparable names.

Being a twin is not unlike being a team—like Burns and Allen, Martin and Lewis, Nichols and May. It is December 1957, and Deane and I are at school backstage trying not to throw up. Tonight we will perform a sister act. We hoist our plump legs into the hoop of chiffon clouds. We are wearing another one of our mother's chiffon concoctions—the cupped sleeves, the full skirts—that make us look even plumper, like good lemon puddings. The teacher hauls us across the stage, pausing to part the center curtains and shove us through. Deane takes my hand, and we squint into the spotlight. Even before we start, there is laughter.

"The Twins," we recite. "In form and feature, face and limb,/ I grew so like my sister./That folks got taking me for her/And each for one another . . ."

We are funny. The fact of us is funny. And without one another, we would get no laughter at all.

We also fight. I take the blouse Deane planned to wear to school. I wave it toward her. I put one arm in a sleeve, staring at her. And then I see her eyes take on their pre-pinch glitter. She springs and I fall on the bed. Her fingernails dig into the skin on the back of my upper arms, printing red crescent moons. Like married people, we have only one fight over and over. We fight about what we never solve for each other. We try to pull the promise of certainty through the pores of each other's skins. *It's got to be in there.* And when it isn't, we fight.

We fight because we are sisters and also because we can't fight with our parents. But the fury Deane and I unleash on each other is also disappointment. We are too fat. We aren't blonde, lithe children who love to join teams. We don't dress right. We take our fingernails and scratch each other's skin for an answer.

The pinches hurt and they bleed. Our nails don't make regular, healthy looking cuts. These are brighter pink. When I am in school looking down at my book I see the curve on my forearm. It cuts across my freckles: Deane angry on my arm. I think how we go at each other until we roll up like fighting cats, until one of us breaks loose. I see Deane fly at me, and I know her pinch will hurt, and once her hands are on me, the pinch won't stop until she is through my skin.

Afterward, we examine each other's pinches. We get out Band-Aids and long-sleeve shirts. We don't want friends to see. But they do. A drop of blood bleeds through the white oxford shirts we wear to school. The bright raw place not just scraped skin but blood on a shirt.

We are not yet keen to know who we are. A scratch on my arm from

Deane is the same as a self-inflicted one. We are each other, and that's enough. No one matters to us as much as we do to each other. We live in a neighborhood of big, old houses and recessed lawns with few children. On snow days, the Loeshe boys come from far down the street to Roach's hill, the Spahrs and the Rileys from the top of a drive we can't see, the Forsters from their books. But we don't play with them: they are younger or boys, or live on the out-of-bounds side of the street. It doesn't matter. Each day I wake up, and Deane is there. We grab our stick horses and ride the plains. We are cowboys, and our horses rear and run backward. We run until the edge of sky over Kellogg's field burns pink, a chill cuts through us, tomorrow school, and no more horses, dark in our gallop home.

Chapter 21

We decide to have the funeral on Wednesday, August 26, and we are in time's slow drag. My life seems a long field to pass through, groping toward Deane. I decide the end of life is when I get to have her back, and the time in between is senseless. I feel uselessly young, so many decades between Deane and me.

On Tuesday, my mother and I go shopping because I brought no funeral dress from Tennessee. I buy a lavender floral with a lace collar, Deane's favorite color, the first dress I see, the one I know is right. I do not try it on.

The store is the store of our childhood, where Deane and I took our allowance to spend, where we went with our mother to buy look-alike dresses, where she ran her hand between the waistbands and our plump stomachs. My mother hands the dress to the sales lady.

"My daughter just died. We are shopping for her funeral," my mother says, supposing that our chaos hovers over us, plain as a printed sign.

"Mom." I tug at her sleeve. Her revelation embarrasses me, as if she had put both our hearts on the counter. I want to snatch mine back.

"Oh. I'm so sorry," says the sales lady, who stares at us, wary now of what we might expose her to.

"Purple was her favorite," my mother keeps on, fingering the dress. "The funeral's tomorrow, and this daughter"—she gestures toward me—"has nothing to wear."

I cannot tell my mother to stop her manic cheerfulness. The world outside us, the world of the quotidian, has turned foreign, and this is how she passes through it.

Dan does not come with us on our shopping trip, but he is there for everything else. He is not a talker. He slips in and sits beside us in the den, and he brings us drinks and cheese and crackers. He answers the phone and keeps up with the dishes. He slides next to me and gives me reason to feel that I may remain on earth, his presence my presence. When the minister comes, Dan answers the door. Later, he tells me how struck he was by Warren's cheerfulness, "a good thing," he says. He writes a thank-you for my mother, one she cannot write, she says, but has to, to say something about kindness. He does this best, sitting in the living room, a blank white sheet on top of his book, the words spread with graciousness for my mother. He stamps it, and it's done. He sets the table with my Aunt Po, laying out silver for guests who will fill the room after the funeral. But he and I hardly speak. We don't need to.

Wednesday, I wake early to harsh voices and see huge crows moving over the lawn, black contrasts to a vivid sky. They are messengers from Deane, and I look for them everywhere.

Dan and I are sleeping in my brother's room, where the images of Deane and me are not so vivid as they would be in our old room. I stand at the window in my nightgown, watching the crows take off and land again on the willow tree. Against the sky, they look certain of everything, and their shrieks convince me that they carry the knowledge I'm after. Later I learn that ancient cultures believed crows ferried the souls of the dead, and I think, *No wonder.*

I spend much of my time staring out this window, any window, looking for what has changed. But the yard is the same. It's what I know that has altered. Our history, which lies in the trees, the street asphalt, the neighbors' lawns, now also holds, reveals the future. The story's there like a tarp pegged down on four sides: the future over an eclipsing past. Deane's death always there, the fact we ran toward on stick horses.

We go to the church early for a family viewing. Deane's body lies before us in her fuchsia dress. I lean to kiss her cheek, a doll's face, hard and cool. Wherever she is, she is not here. I place her soft gray turtleneck, jeans, thick Earth shoes beside her. I add a box of Russell Stover chocolates and a sheaf of my poetry. I write her a letter. I shut my insides down like a neighborhood store, lower the awning, slam home the accordion gate. This is not happening to me, this is not happening to me, this is not happening to me.

At 1:30 a limo arrives.

"Make this a happy day," says my uncle, his expression one of possibility and salute.

I am wearing my new purple dress, the dress I think of as Deane's dress, not one I would have picked except for her. I am a confusion of her colors. At the church—the same church where we sang in short Christmas skirts—I cross the green lawn to waiting friends who enclose me, a blurry swarm of mourners, and for a moment I feel safe or loved or both. I could just as easily be getting married. My family, Dan, and I go in the side door to the vestibule. Beyond its inner door, the sanctuary is packed like Easter with flowers and people. We slip into the front pews and before us lies Deane's oak casket, enormous, closed.

The service begins at 3 o'clock, and soon Warren nods at me. Danny and I climb to the podium. Danny steps behind, but I reach back for his hand and pull him closer so I can feel him behind me. I look out on the faces and begin to speak. I am Deane's record keeper, and I have to get it right.

"She had many names," I begin. "I mention this first because for so many years no one knew what her name was—Deane or Dorothy . . . "

I start with her name, her nicknames, the names I gave her, the names she wanted—Clo, Cloie, Madge. Names are freighted matter for twins. Fooling with a name, abbreviating it, rhyming it, twisting it into a nickname: all that a singleton takes for granted is a twin's gift.

"And then one new name: Dr. Deane . . . "

"She used to worry that she was too quiet a person. I never found her quiet. But she said sometimes she had trouble talking. She said, 'Doe, where do all your words come from?'"

I talk about the quiet that worried her, defined her. I envied her ability to keep her mouth shut. I couldn't begin to guess how she did it. I want her stillness.

I feel my hands shake, and I lay my wrists on the pulpit to steady them.

"To Dad, know who I am. I am so much you. To Mom, my hand is in your hand. . . . To me, we will be together forever. . . . "

My voice does not shake; I know what I am doing and that I am the one to do it. I speak for Deane, and I say goodbye to each person she loved. The words are Deane's so saying them is easy

"I made a promise to Deane that if anything ever happened to her, I would be all right. That is what she wants for all of us. 'People have enormous resilience,' she would say. 'Time does work.' And that is what she will give us still: herself, and all the time we need."

When the service ends, Deane's lover, former husband, friends, brother, and cousins carry out her coffin. I cannot take my eyes from the polished wood. We go out the side door and step into the yard where a burial pit waits for us to stand at its edge. My brother and I nod at each other, to Warren. The casket lowers into the ground, and I lose my breath. Surely we do not have to bury her, but I cannot think what else to do.

Chapter 22

Until the seventh grade, Deane and I dress alike, and in every class we sit one behind the other, like a blur in the row. But when we transfer to a private all-girls school for junior high, *everyone* dresses alike in green pleated uniforms that end no more than six inches above our knees. (Before morning assemblies, teachers ask students to kneel so that they can measure the length with a yardstick.) In that sea of green, Deane and I are parted, assigned to different classrooms. Now, like every other girl in the class, I am just one.

When we enter that school in September we are among the shortest. By June we are among the tallest. In nine months, we have grown eight inches. I buy a brown watch-plaid dress with a wide black patent leather buckle. My brother points to my waist.

"When'd you get that?"

Deane and I stop gnawing square crackers into gun shapes, we stop hiding food under the sofa. It becomes our purpose in life to eat as little as possible, to eat only standing up when calories don't count, and to have the skinniest legs on earth. None of these things happen. We are hungry all the time. We get home from school and eat bagsful of cookies and skip dinner. We lie on our beds doing our homework, sucking butterscotch. We drink Metracal, a chalky meal substitute. Our father, who worries about his own weight constantly, stands in our doorway and insists we come to dinner. We sit at the dining room table, but we won't eat. The line of his lips flattens.

"Girls, if you don't eat protein, if you don't drink enough milk, your bones won't grow. If you don't have your health, you don't have anything."

"I'm not hungry," I say.

"I ate when I got home," Deane says.

He puts a bottle of multivitamins on the table and talks about the importance of a banana's potassium to our hearts.

"I starved myself in high school, and I did ruin my health," he says. "I wanted to play football. But I never could. You girls are just too skinny."

We pick at our plates. Our mother who, at five-feet-nine weighs 145, the most she has ever weighed, doesn't say a word. She likes thin.

"You can't be too rich or too thin," she's fond of repeating. Dad blames her.

"Deane, I want to eat dinner together in the dining room. The girls have got to eat."

She repeats this to us, but we know she doesn't care.

Deane and I weren't anorexic, but we sure used food to square off with our father. Jeff's rebellion is more straightforward. He fights with our father, thrusting his chin into Dad's face. By the time he is sixteen, his life takes place apart from us. He lies on his bed, his door locked, talking on the phone to his girlfriend, Margie. Or he sits in a boat on the Schuylkill River, dragging oars to his chest and pushing them away. When our father travels—which is much of the time—our mother, afraid of burglars, sleeps in our brother's room so that she can lock us all in one tidy unit. Deane and I hear them talking.

"But why do girls say no," asks our brother.

"You are too young for girls," says our mother.

"Awww, Ma," Jeff answers in a kind of resignation and despair.

The next day Mom asks Jeff to take out the garbage.

He walks past her into the den. "Later," he mutters.

"You will too do it now," she says, flinging her forearm after him as if it's a rope that can circle his neck. He runs, and she chases him.

Yiiiiiiii, he cries as he wraps his body in a down comforter and sprints through his room and ours.

She cannot catch him. Winding around the corners, he slams the doors between them and keeps up his circles until he slips and falls on the bed and she leans over him with a hairbrush and hits him through the down over and over until he is crying not from pain but from the wrath that steams from her face.

In pictures before we are born, Jeff is always with our mother. In those pictures lies their happiness, his certainty that she will not release him, hers that he doesn't want to go. But now they have a different posture. As our brother moves through his teens, he shuts the door in all our faces. Our mother sits on the sofa in the den and watches old Westerns, pouring a little scotch in her Coke.

That year my English teacher eats meanness. She makes me recite twelve verses of *La Belle Dame Sans Merci*. The bell rings at verse eleven. Miss Moses plugs a black curl behind her ear and looks at me. "*You can start over tomorrow.*"

She likes wisecrackers, popular girls whose bosoms push at their pleats. Having her as a teacher is like having a mean girl take over the school. I want to tell on her, but whom would I tell? Miss Watson, the Bible teacher, believes in the Holy Ghost, but she won't believe this.

I tell no one. Instead I make the first friend I have ever had to myself. Her name is Cynthia, and no one else likes her. She has buckteeth, and the other girls say she talks too much. Even the mean teacher makes fun of her. That only makes me like Cynthia more. She has a laugh that makes her head tilt and wobble. She wears headbands and lives on a farm and likes her mother, who also has buckteeth and a big laugh. Cynthia sits with me on the bus to the hockey field and invites me to play at her house at the end of the first week. I am so excited that I forget about Deane, who cries in the bathroom because she wasn't invited.

This invite is the first for just me, and the singleness rattles in my head like a marble. I let my mother comfort Deane, and I go to Cynthia's where we walk around cow ponds, past ducks, over rocks. We play Parcheesi, and I win lots of real estate. We eat graham crackers at her kitchen table, dunking them in cold milk. But I am only partly there, uneasy, a tin echo in my stomach. Why am I here, scuffing my shoes in cow dung? This feeling I will have for the rest of my life. I am apart, and the events around me read like the lit ticker tape the Philadelphia *Evening Bulletin* runs around the corners of its building. I am not quite present. This is something to get through. One more glass of milk and I get to go home. Two more houses in Parcheesi. Five more steps to the car. And when the door slams, there's Deane in the backseat and my mom, her *L'Air du Temps*. Without Deane, I am only a set of phrases and movements, waiting for some echo to still. A twin's intimacy is an expensive lesson: how far away our selves lie from the world that scares us. When I go home, Deane and I make a bowl of popcorn, sharing it on the floor while we read. A piece of me snaps back in place.

We are becoming more like Yin and Yang than Tweedledee and Twee-dledum. Deane is far quieter than I am, more studious, cerebral, and pri-vate. She has moved into the guest room. Shortly before that, she'd wakened me with her early morning studies.

"Turn that light off," I grumble, slamming my head under the pillow.

"I'm studying," she says without looking at me, her head in the book.

"Sleep counts too," I mutter, rolling over. She's laughing now but keeps studying.

I don't want her to get ahead of me, so I get up and study too. She has become my model of diligence. I'm after more fun. But if she studies hard, I have to too.

She has a seriousness I begin to ponder. Its mystery worries me. I'm not quite sure who this Deane is if not exactly me. I am tempestuous, impulsive, quick to anger, and her calm infuriates and confuses me.

But I like having my own room, and I like running into Deane's room in the mornings to get her. I look at her one morning as she combs her hair facing the mirror and wonder if she is prettier than me. I am think-ing that she is, that I want to be more like her. To an outsider, of course, those feelings sound like a ridiculous farce. But I find myself for the first time jealous of Deane. She has a certainty I don't.

On Friday nights, we again stand in front of the mirror combing our hair. To the left. To the right. Our mother has enrolled us in dance class.

The good part is that we get to buy ballroom dresses with little straps. The bad part is that we have to hold hands with sweaty boys and push ourselves around a ballroom like broomsticks. Most of the boys can't speak. Our tongues too thicken and die.

Our dance teachers are a silver-haired man and his beautiful partner who happens to be our neighbor. She is Hollywood slim with jet-black curly hair. Her red chiffon skirt sashays forward and sideways as he twists her backward through the room, sliding together as easily as Bill and Ginger. She looks happy. She is laughing. She's Sally's mother but not like any mother we know.

They make us do what they do. All the floating lifts and dips, the side-steps and slides. But we are sticks with bowed heads and leaden feet. I am paired with Howard, who has hot hands, curly black hair, and braces, and I am afraid my cheek will touch his. Deane spins away with Don. He is tall and thin, but he is one of the boys whose penis gets pinched by other boys. Deane slides away, Don's hand at her back, and I can feel its wetness.

But we are saved. The classes stop. The silver man runs away with our friend's mother. She leaves our street, her five children, her tall prince-like husband, their grand house on the hill. She lets her hair drop out of a window, climbs down it, and marries the dancing teacher. Her daughter comes to school, but we can't talk to her. What would we say? Her mother fell in love in front of all of us. Even now, her face the face of happiness. We thought they were dancing in a box step, but they were dancing to paradise.

Another mother starts another class the next year in a different building, for which we have to be interviewed and invited by society ladies. We dress up in satin formals, line up along the wall, and wait for a boy to ask us to dance. The lights are off, the heat is up, and the music thumps. I have my hair in a French twist and my mother's rouge on my cheeks. I have no breasts to flatten, but my dress has them sewn in like markers of where I'm supposed to be. Some of the girls are elegant, not at all like the saddle-shoed lot at school. Joan has breasts and straight, white teeth locked in a retainer. We know Joan kisses boys. Sometimes, we see the stage curtains rustle, and she's back there with the big blond boy from Episcopal. We are frozen by the possibility. This dancing on Fridays is something we can't say no to—like liquid vitamins or booster shots. We too could be backstage but to get there requires this knowledge: popularity is a gauntlet of sweaty hands and bad breath in strangled throats. Get past those and you get to step into a person different from the one you are. You can almost see her: the better, magazine you. This is what we box-step for.

If you don't get picked, a woman with bosoms flattened by stiff fabric pulls you to the center and puts your hand in a boy's hand. A tall, thin, good-looking boy goes to Deane. A short, stocky, freckled-faced boy comes to me. Mr. Good Looks' draw to Deane only makes me more certain that she is moving away from me, that she has something I don't have. She is becoming someone I don't know, separate from me.

After the dance is over, my sister and I wait outside in the cold air that dries our perspiration into salt at the side of our faces. Our mother pulls up in the car, and we glide back into normality, the most graceful step this evening, into our mother's version of things, her smoky car, her red lips, her safe real bosom not sewn to anything, and her dancing feet that don't gallivant off with the dance teacher.

That night, Deane and I giggle on my bed.

"His hands were wet," she says.

"I know. Howard's were too."

"And the side of his face."

"You touched the side of his face?"

"He asked me to a dance at Episcopal."

"Do you think anyone will ask me? I'm so jealous." I start to cry.

"I don't know whether to go."

I take hope and stop crying.

"Go."

"I don't want to go without you. But I do. Please don't cry. Maybe Howard will ask you."

We both start to laugh, disgusted.

"First one up wakes the other one up," Deane says.

By the time we go to high school we have figures and have learned how to keep our hair from moving, red flips stuck to our heads like Dutch caps. And our notice of boys—creatures who like to talk about football or nothing at all—has ramped up. Who are they exactly? We explore via Ted, a short, skinny boy whose huge glasses cover his face. From Ted, who sits in front of us in homeroom, we learn boys can be funny and un-scary. But we also know that Ted isn't scary because he isn't sexy.

Our sophomore year is sterile. Deane and I make the same friends, friends who are as baffled by boys are we are. We wear red lipstick and a perfume called *Blue Grass*, and we go to sleepovers at our best friend Allison's, who wears a black curler cap that tells us she knows more about sex than we do. She and Sue, our other best friend, tell all. Deane and I are horrified, certain our parents are excluded from what the pair describe. Now we are certain we want nothing to do with boys. But in our high school we meet the only other set of twins we've known: Joan and Jane. They are not identical so there is always debate about who is prettier, sexier. Both of them have bosoms and waists: think Jennifer Anniston in the sixties. As our mother said wryly, "They do seem older."

All the boys want them. So we study them, and we study them hard. What do they have that the boys want? We can't exactly say, but we feel it too, an allure, a mystery. Even the senior boys want them, particularly Joan. And we think they want her because she is more distant, cooler in tone than her warmer, friendlier sister. *You can't have me, but you can try.* And all the boys wanted to try.

One boy who tries is Bill. He dates Joan and then Jane and then has his heart broken. Bill *is* sexy, Deane and I both like him, and we are astounded by the other twins' rejection. But lucky for us, Bill has apparently learned nothing from his first twin go-round: he asks first one of us out and then the other. For a while Deane and I are content to share him. It's fun to talk together about how dreamy his blue eyes are, how sexy his slow, wide smile. (Think brawnier Tom Cruise.) But then we see the pattern that needs to stop. If Bill can't decide, we'll decide for him. We flip a coin, and Deane wins. And I start dating Bill's best friend.

This is not a story of generous sisters but of two girls who know that without help, people cannot decide between them. Although we do not *feel* interchangeable, the world blinks when it sees us, and so we lend a hand. With Bill we begin to learn a strategy for distinction. One of us will withdraw.

Even if we don't know it, this is the start of separation: like one tree, we splinter off into separate branches. Deane moves into love: I see her kissing Bill and wonder who she is, what she feels. She tries out for the tennis team, and she's good at it, loves it. To me, tennis is a game where people bend over picking up balls. I start to read poetry, Matthew Arnold and e.e. Cummings. I start to write, so much easier than speaking. I can get things clear, work them until I get them right. I can sound braver than I feel. I can be anyone. Deane is obsessed with algebra, with working like a boll weevil for Dr. Copeland, the hardest teacher in the school. He gives pop tests, and Deane is always sick just before his class. She's scared, but she aces it. That's Deane. She runs for student council, and when the vote is cast, I am busy painting props for an English class presentation.

"I lost by one vote," Deane says. She looks at me, her eyes angry and sad—mine the vote.

"Oh, I am so sorry."

She shrugs, about to cry, what no one wants to do at school.

"She didn't mean to, Deanie," my mother says later at home, on both our sides at the same time.

We have Allison and Sue over for the Beatles' debut on Ed Sullivan. We dress in black turtlenecks, our hair combed forward. We scream and sing in the Sardine Lounge while our parents laugh.

"Is that really singing?" my father asks, shaking his head. My mother passes popcorn and beats hot fudge to pour on a buttered plate.

I think about romance all the time. I am in love with Paul McCartney, and I stare at his brown eyes while I play his songs that I record off the radio.

"How can I marry him?" I ask Deane.

Deane is busy building B-I-L-L in three dimensions on her notebook.

"Maybe Dad could help," she says absently.

I turn up the radio, roll over toward the snowy window.

Deane and I still have the same friends, go to the same sleepovers, wear the same clothes. But we now have what Matthew Arnold calls *buried lives*, the ones we can't explain to ourselves, let alone each other. A year from now we don't even know where we'll be, I think, as I write one more college essay. Deane and I apply to all the same schools, get in the same ones, get rejected by the same ones. We have the same numerical rank in our class. But we know we are headed, if only metaphorically, to different places.

By my senior year, I am sick of dating Bill's friends. I have noticed a tall, thin boy with black, curly hair and thick glasses with black frames. I do what I now realize all girls do: I tell someone. That night when my dad calls me to the phone, a deep voice introduces itself as Scott. And I fall in love.

I ask my mother what she would think if I loved a Jewish boy. To her it's a theoretical question.

"It's harder for people with different backgrounds," she says cryptically.

But the mystery he embodies is part of what I'm drawn to. He lives in the Jewish part of town.

"The soul station quits when you get to Gladwyne," he teases me about my white Christian suburb. His family calls me Scott's *shiksa*, the name for a non-Jewish woman who has attracted a Jewish man. Scott's mother buys him deli butter cookies filled with jam or dipped in chocolate, nothing like the Pepperidge Farm cookies we eat at home.

Each day I wake up in a kind of euphoria, the headiness of new love. And the happier I become, the less I can tell my mother. She finally catches Scott and me kissing by the back door one day before he leaves— a kiss I remember, long and lovely—and she claps her hands at us.

"None of that," she says. "Time to go home, Scott."

She asks Deane and me to tell Bill and Scott not to use the tiny bathroom next to the Sardine Lounge.

"I don't want you to hear them urinating," she says.

"Want to step outside, Bill?" Scott asks Bill from then on, the two of them laughing.

But it isn't funny, this new puritanical mother who seems both angry and frightened by our newly found desires. I am angry back. She seems maybe a little crazy, I think, now that she is darkly suspicious, refusing to go upstairs when the boys are over, sending our father downstairs to make sure the lights are on. I don't like this new mother. For the first time I wonder why my parents sleep in twin beds like couples on TV.

From the outset, Scott makes it clear that he knows who I am. His call is not the result of deliberations about Deane and me. Nor does he show much curiosity about Deane. He is nice to her but only because she is my sister. She holds no magic for him. *I do.*

I don't just quietly observe this. I question Scott closely: *Could he fall in love with Deane? What does he like about me? Does he think I am prettier?* (He is the first person to tell me that I have a clearer, more animated face than Deane, a description it takes me years to understand. What's a hazy face?) He says he chooses me because of the way I love to talk, because of my frankness, because he thinks I'm pretty and smart. And because of that, I share with him what I have only shared with Deane: intimacy.

If intimacy is a kind of geography, then Scott is a new map. He tells me what it means to be Jewish, his view on nuns, what boys think about sex. He smokes Marlboros and eats Milano cookies simultaneously, and he wears Aqua de Silva. We lie on my parents' couch, and he takes his glasses off, and we kiss. All the lessons of my parents and the secrets with my sister and the language of books and movies no longer are as real or true as Scott's brown eyes. At seventeen, we are alone, and not even Deane knows how much I love him. And because I understand close-ness, this map is easy to navigate. As I venture across its territory, I have begun to change from a twin into a person apart from Deane.

That fall, Deane and I leave home while Bill heads south and Scott stays in Philadelphia. We go to Tufts University in Medford, Massachusetts, where we live in the same dorm (we can wave to each other from our windows) and take the same classes. We no longer dress alike, but we share clothes, and our confused roommates never know who stands in their closets at 7 o'clock in the morning picking out skirts.

We are the only twins on a small campus, and we stick out. Glad to be together in a place full of strangers, we are always each other's first choice: it is Deane I want to explore Boston with, go shopping with, eat meals with. But we begin to see that our closeness is a barrier: people have trouble coming close, and we have trouble letting them. Because what interests people about us—our sameness—is no longer what we want them to be interested in. If they can't get past our faces, they can't know who we are—and neither can we. We feel more urgency here, now that we have left home where our mother at least knew us apart, inside and out. And it is only our parents we've left; until we leave each other we're not, like our peers, truly away. The thirst for independence spurs us—and the knowledge that we can't be together forever, not if we want families of our own, lives of our own. After all, nothing we're doing feels easy: who doesn't find it warmer in her mother's kitchen, eating hot milk toast on a cold morning?

In some ways our mother made leaving easier: her constantly expressed desire that we come home only made us realize that we couldn't go back without suffocating. As we separate from her, we also see more clearly how unhappy she is with our critical father. She is all appetite, a woman who loves to smoke, eat, and drink. She tells me, "I'd be happy wearing jeans and eating hotdogs," dismissing the more glamorous life of cocktail parties and balls that Dad feels his work requires. At the dinner table, when Dad has our attention, she glowers at him for stealing us. Sometimes, she gets up without saying a word and slowly walks up the stairs. I can even see anger pulsing in the disappearing calves.

When we go home that first Christmas, she can't leave us alone, follows us from room to room, complains when we go out with friends, not something our other friends' parents do. I feel sorry for her and furious with her all at once. When Deane and I head to a library to write term papers, I feel I can finally breathe.

"Don't grow away from me," Mom says to me one morning, standing in my doorway.

"I'm not," I snap, turning away.

All the good stuff—the independence, the chance to figure out who you are, the man you'll live with—none of that happens until you leave home.

And Deane too is home. Even our peers know our split is overdue. Still, I compound the problem our second year. I develop a thyroid infection that keeps me in Philadelphia for two weeks at the start of the fall term. The easiest path is to ask Deane to sign me up for all the same classes she does. So, when I return, we move in lockstep, sharing teachers and class-mates, sitting next to each other, moving from class to class like one blurry image.

One day we overhear a boy in our psychology class ask his friend why we would ever want to go to school together. He asks this as if we are freaks. Out there, coming at us like a train on schedule, is an insistence on separation. We can see it, a funnel fuming over flat land. We are re-luctant and angry and confused. But we see it coming.

Chapter 23

Palmer doesn't matter.

Until September 30, when a man delivering oil to a winter home deep in the Vermont woods finds Palmer's car. The next morning, a search party spreads out into the woods, combing its brush for six hours. They move from farmhouse to farmhouse, talking to the people who live there. They find nothing.

Until October 18, when the phone rings, my parents, one on each extension. It's the FBI. Two bow-and-arrow hunters have found Palmer's body in the woods of Barnard, Vermont.

His route was simple. He drove to Pomfret, a town next to Barnard, over a covered bridge on winding, gravel roads until he came to a pasture high with summer grasses. He lifted a cable barring his way onto an old power-line road, rocky and steep. Six feet past the cable, the car got stuck. He climbed from his car and walked four miles into the woods, past a white-frame farmhouse, into a field until he came to a stone wall, a spot that seemed right for another shooting.

A single gunshot to his head.

I am standing in the kitchen when my parents call to tell us, the receiver tucked under my chin. I will never have to meet my sister's murderer or share a courtroom with him. I will not hear him speak. I will not have to see his family or the Stoney Brook families.

I read an article about a woman whose sister was murdered. Again and again the woman attended parole hearings of her sister's murderer, certain, yet troubled, that her vote against his release kept him in prison.

"When Mumbaugh killed my sister, he put a knife into my family's heart," wrote the woman.

I see the film *Witness* about a Quaker boy who sees a murder. The boy's grandfather talks to him about violence, asks his grandson if he would kill another human being.

"Only the bad ones."

"And you can recognize this bad man?"

"Yes, I have seen him."

"And seeing him, you become him?"

I do not want to know who I can become. I do not want to make Palmer matter.

Palmer got a gun permit when he was twenty-five, three years before he stepped into Deane's office, a permit that lasts five years, that allows buying several guns. He chose the .357 magnum left beside Deane's body and another he carried for his own death. He liked bullets that "would blow out the back, coming out," he told a friend.

He shot Deane and Alan Shields execution-style. At close range. He left so much blood, at first no one could tell where the wounds were.

I look at his newspaper photo, his straight brown hair, his sad round face and dark eyes, his mouth disguised by a boomerang mustache. He was, one of Deane's colleagues speculates, a paranoid schizophrenic— his life sentence, his family's too. Years later, I call Lowell information to find his mother's phone number. I want to see her face, to hear about her son, to understand the inexplicable.

"The family was well known and highly regarded," says the *Boston Globe*.

Mrs. Palmer's phone number is unlisted. I am not surprised: the day of the shootings, a crank caller phoned her home, sobbing into the phone, pretending he was Palmer. Police guarded her and Palmer's wife and child. As if the police could keep them safe, as if erasure were possible.

Unlisted, Mrs. Palmer is absent. She is not there for reporters. Or lawyers. Or the wail of someone pretending to be her son. How did her face change? As mine did?

What strikes me now is that Palmer's story is so ordinary, American ordinary. James Francis Palmer: a five-feet-eleven, 170-pound high school athlete called *Jim* who marries his high school sweetheart. Chelmford High's Outstanding Senior Athlete, 1972. Captain and MVP Varsity Hockey. Outstanding running back. Baseball player. Who plays horseshoes in his backyard at midnight. Whose hobby is target shooting. A friendly, quiet guy, his friends say: *One of the nicest kids you ever want to know. A smart kid. He must've gone off the deep end.*

Palmer goes to prep school for a year after high school and has a bloody fight with his roommate Mark, whom he blames for a prank Mark didn't do. Just after the shooting, Mark is afraid Palmer will come for him.

Palmer graduates in criminal justice from Northeastern University in Boston, completing the program a year early to try for a police job to follow his father, once police chief and dead at forty-four.

In 1980, Palmer goes to California to work as a security guard for a few months. In September and again in October, the Los Angeles police tell him that, although he passed the police exam, they have to deny his application because he has hearing problems, he's overweight, he has high blood pressure. He sends his wife cashier's checks. He takes a class that trains him to use firearms. He abandons his mother's car in Nevada, its innards shot. Jobless, he goes back to Lowell in October to work for another security company that fires him in June. His life disintegrates like the car he abandons.

Three weeks before the shootings, he calls the Lowell police chief to find out how fast he is moving up the reserve list, how fast he could become the policeman that would make him safe, us safe. But he leaves one part of his application unfinished: the requirement for psychological testing, added in 1980. He shows up for some tests but not for others. Until he does, the department says, it will not employ him.

I want to know him. At first I stare at those brown eyes for an answer. One of Deane's former colleagues had speculated that he might have been paranoid schizophrenic. I look up the term. Palmer was not alone:

one person in every ten thousand is diagnosed with schizophrenia. Its types are as varied as cereal choices: catatonic schizophrenia, disorganized schizophrenia, residual schizophrenia, and, of course, the one that may have found Palmer in his late teens or early twenties, a boy making his way, dreaming of becoming a police officer like his father.

Paranoid schizophrenics seize a theme, a tune of persecution to play over and over. Palmer had themes to choose from: he was a man who my sister said dressed like a woman, a man who wanted to be a policeman. But at the Lowell Police Department, he didn't make the cut. People there gave him a gun for intermittent security work, but he hadn't worked for them for at least two years, his name on the waiting list for a permanent assignment. What did they know? What did his application show? What shredded speech gave them the clues to turn him down, the son of a police chief?

He told my sister—and perhaps Dr. Shields—that he dressed like a woman, and when he couldn't see his way to the spot his father owned, whom else could he blame?

Paranoid schizophrenics hear what haunts them. *I can't be on the force because they know my secret. I can't be on the force because they told what no one knows. I can't be on the force because my head is exploding with shame and anger and nothing that makes sense.*

Several weeks before the murders he tells his friend Bob how angry he is at Shields and Deane, that they're the ones who got him fired. And that his sister and Bob were behind it too. When Bob goes to Palmer's house one day that summer, Palmer fights with his wife, breaking a glass, shoving his mother. He can't sleep. He wants to leave the country. The day before the murders he plays tennis with Bob. He had the night shift, he tells Bob, but he would meet him for tennis at noon the next day. Whatever Palmer did was planned, Bob says.

I can't pretend to understand what was real for Palmer and what wasn't. I don't know at what point Shields and Deane became synonymous with Palmer's anger and shame—and a solution for them: stanch them, stanch his demons. In his hauntedness, did he kill them over and over, so often, that like Macbeth he had nothing to lose by stepping over the boundary of fantasy? "I am in blood, stepped in so far that should I wade no more, Returning were as tedious as go'oer," says Macbeth of his murders. There is a dark joke about revelation: *I can't tell you because then I will have to kill you.* That became Palmer's burden: nothing could erase his secret except his doctors' deaths.

Chapter 24

Division. Our first step: we spend the summer of our sophomore year apart, Deane in France and I in Switzerland. It is our first separation of more than a few days, and we are nineteen years old.

My adoptive family—mother; father; Mireille, six; Janine, fourteen; and Gilbert, sixteen—comes to pick me up at the train station in Lausanne. They stand, tiny and ruddy-cheeked, holding a placard: *Dorothy Foltz*, and I forge toward them, watching myself in a European film, adopted by shy strangers in dark, worn clothing. I climb into their car, and we head to Rommanel-sur-Morges, a town of farmers outside Lausanne. I am the family's guest and their live-in help—although they all work harder than I do. The first day, I pick beans in the garden beside their house and sew them together with needle and thread to hang in lines from hot attic beams. All afternoon my stomach turns. I want to sit down, close my eyes, be home. I keep working, ignorant of what will happen in the next hour, or even the next minute. I am like a dog watching its master. When he moves, I get up and follow, but I am not sure where we are going or why.

At night, I climb into a feather bed and listen to cowbells clank below my window. The house is mocha stucco with thick walls and dark, cool hallways. The overgrown yard swallows up the house, and when I look out the window, the cows hunch next to the house, unbudging. But I am not a happy traveler, animated by foreignness and surprise. I am an intruder. Fatigue saves me. My bones ache from bending to pick beans. At 6 a.m. Madame wakes me, *Reveillez. Bon jour,* and my French sits logged in my chest refusing to rise. *Hello, hello,* I say. *Bon jour.*

I begin a ritual of breakfast. I go downstairs in my shapeless black-and-yellow shift and take a crusty loaf from the wood breadbox, cutting a slab to eat with strawberry jam and hot tea—my favorite part of the day, sitting in the empty kitchen enjoying my respite. If Madame comes in, the moment sours because I do not know the norm. Am I the shiftless American, supping while others work? When she enters, no matter my meal, I am finished. She is all business, setting a few cans on the windowsill for the garbage collector, pulling raw chicken from the icebox for the noon meal. I watch her brown-lined face, her ubiquitous worried look.

The breadbox is empty, and I walk down the hall to the one-room grocery at the back of the house. There the baker has already dumped a dozen loaves in the bread bin. I pick a new one, warm and crusty, cutting in. Madame teaches me how to manage the store, to make change, to run the cash register. I begin to feel the quiet lie like a cloth over my heart. I sit at the counter on a stool learning to count Swiss coins into the villagers' hands. The older women, dressed in long, black dresses, ask Madame who I am, as if I am not quite there. And it's true that I am mute, partly because my French is not good but also because fear chokes me. I do not know how to speak about a fear I don't understand.

I begin hiding peanuts and *petit beurres* next to my bed because the meals bewilder me. I never know what is coming, and in Switzerland it is rude not to take seconds, not to eat everything on your plate. So each night I take very little, certain many courses will follow. On some nights I am right: we eat soup and rabbit and gravy and *pommes frites* and fresh yogurt from the dairy down the road. But on others, we have only soup and bread, and I do not get enough food until later, under the eiderdown, where I get plenty. So I am gaining weight. On their scale I weigh 60 kilos, then 62, then 65. I wear loose dresses and despise my body, my loneliness. How much do I know about separation and sadness, about a beginning of what most terrifies me?

Every day I wait for the mail. Madame carries it into the hall. *Dorothe*, she calls, and there is a thin blue letter from Deane in France. She writes about her rich French family, the handsome father, the quiet, sweet daughter who befriends her, the welcoming mother, the mad maid who, on Deane's arrival, points repeatedly to her own vagina until Deane realizes she is offering the toilet. Deane is learning to drink wine. And she too is getting fat. On boat rides down the Seine, Deane wears the same shapeless crepe dresses I do.

I mark the days until I can go home. Each afternoon I walk with six-year-old Mireille to the dairy down the road. The pigs line up against the fence, fighting for the trough. They stink. They make stink visible. They turn Swiss blue sky into odor, an object we walk through to get to cheese. Inside the small, white dairy building, the smell is gone. The walls and floor are scrubbed and pure, and wheels of Gruyere sit on chrome counters. Mireille hands her bucket to the dairyman so he can fill it with sweet yogurt. But even as I stand inside this strange, wondrous life, which goes on day after day whether I am here or not, I cannot stop wondering if *my* world still exists. Everything I know is gone, replaced by yogurt and cheese and string beans and French sentences that float past me, inscrutable.

All day I wonder where Deane is. I picture her happy, drinking wine, sailing, swimming. I am jealous. I want to be with Deane, and I want to be Deane.

Most people have felt what I feel that summer, going out into the world apart from their families, bewildered about who they are now, apart. But in our case the bewilderment is exaggerated. We don't have the practice, say, from the first day of kindergarten of leaving everyone we know behind. Deane is always there. Neither of us walk into a room alone and have to find our way. For others, separation repeats, repeats until they understand that departing is as the Irish song describes: *Goodbye love, there's no one leaving.* When we leave home at seventeen, our parents shuffling back to their cars, the other girls go in alone, but Deane and I are only a hallway apart. Now, in Switzerland, I see that the other girls on the trip are learning the same things I am: how to be on their own, how to make their place in our group, how to know who they are. But unlike them, I am waiting for Deane. My body is waiting. My fear and my heart wait. And none of what I encounter feels quite real without her. I am silent because a part of me simply doesn't fire without Deane, a limping engine. But that doesn't matter because I do not know where she is. She is a thin blue airmail sheet that sometimes comes in the mail.

Weeks later, I sit at a café table in Paris, still waiting for Deane. My group is spending its last week here, as is hers. I am happy and restless. I see her coming, and I jump up, and there she is, her arms around me, her smile in mine. The waiter brings us café au lait and croissants, and we can't stop talking. Eating with Deane is like swallowing permission to be present. I have no body and no time because now I am safe. After breakfast we walk along the boulevard and pluck through baskets of sale clothing. I buy an embroidered rust blouse, Deane a pink one. I take her to meet my group, and they scream and laugh at how alike we are. They don't know which of us is which. The familiar confusion calms us. We like it, or at least know we reside there. Confusion is who we are.

Chapter 25

In the fall of 1968, we separate for good, Deane to the University of Pennsylvania and I to Barnard College in New York. A few nights before Deane leaves for Penn, we sort through clothes spread on our brother's bed. We divide like we are divorcing, and we are. We each push favorites on the other, and then we start to cry. We look into a future bare as our closets.

In New York, silence enters me, as it had in Switzerland. Only now I am in a country where I speak the language, and still my days are silent. In the mornings I walk along Broadway to classes, and in the afternoons sit on my bed reading D. H. Lawrence, eating cheddar cheese and crackers. When the weather turns cold, I cross the street from my apartment, open a doorway into a steamy tunnel underneath the college buildings to get to class. I walk past women rolling laundry carts and men hustling dirty dishes to huge dishwashers. Upstairs in a poetry class, Ms. Hall talks about ribald Chaucer while I sit in the back, eating salted raisins in three bites like Charlie Chaplin nibbling crumbs of a roll, hoping they last the whole hour. After class, I walk home, past New York's pink sky into the afternoon smell of burning chocolate. The soot settles on my white coat.

I make one friend, and we do everything together. We jog at an indoor track and eat dinner. We study, we walk to the grocery. Competition is a twin's natural predator. To be "the other" is a solution. Instead of wanting distance, twins want merger. They want the original promise: one egg, one life, one set, completion.

But I am also scared of this woman. She is independent. She is competitive. She is not Deane. She breaks all the rules, the rules twins know by heart that she doesn't know. What she understands as well as I is loneliness, but that is not enough. I expect her to know me, to guess my thoughts. We begin to study at the law school together. But sometimes she leaves before I do. She meets a man, and they leave. Or I am walking down the sidewalk, and she passes me with another friend, and we don't stop. I do not know or understand social distance. Like the dial on a cheap iron, I am only on or off, close or not close, best friends or not friends. To twins, other people are masked, formal, inscrutable. They operate on another set of rules—of distance, request, reserve. They know how to lie, they know how to keep their mouths shut, they know how to be alone.

I begin to dread the weekends, the times when I have no classes, when my silence surrounds me, and my mind becomes a ticker-tape readout of thoughts I can't stop. Saturdays, I push into the city, ride the bus downtown to Fifth Avenue and walk for blocks, looking in windows. I go in Bloomingdale's and get lost and then overwhelmed. Women are pushing through shoes, and the salesmen walk fast, carrying shoeboxes over their heads like entrees. I don't want the sparkling shoes enough to fight for them. I go back down the elevators and sift through socks. I stand shoulder to shoulder with other customers, and for a minute I believe I am still on the sidewalk.

It is late fall. I catch the bus, and as I ride up Fifth into East Harlem across Columbus to West Broadway the day turns dark. My apartment is empty. I have shoved nothing aside. I decide if I feel this way Monday I will go to the school psychologist.

The decision's a frightening one. As I was growing up, the only mention of psychologists came paired with the term *nervous breakdown*. Only really crazy people saw psychologists—like the depressed girl I once saw in a black-and-white school film who lurked behind the curtains in her parents' living room and then had a lobotomy. Mrs. Soloway, our neighbor, had a nervous breakdown when her husband left her for a younger woman. She would come to see my mother, who stood holding her in the dining room. We were very quiet around Mrs. Soloway, who herself became very still. Mrs. Soloway saw psychologists.

But that year in New York, I meet a twenty-seven-year-old graduate student, a man whose family members go to psychologists as often as mine go to the grocery. He himself is in analysis, a daily process, and his talk is full of psychological theory and family patterns and Freud. Of all the people who surround me, he is the only one who understands how much my sadness has to do with Deane. Maybe it would help to talk to someone who understands relationships, he says. He presents the idea like it's a routine physical for my head. I'd sit down, and the shrink would shine a light around my noggin, checking for logjams my sister and I have created. Once he knocks them free, I will step away separate and whole.

But on Monday, routine shores me. I have a schedule. Homework. Classes. Running. Homework. I don't need a shrink. But home alone with the shades down and the black bars over my New York windows, I again feel my self chasing me within a skin I can't escape.

I remember a door plaque I have seen in a classroom building: *Psychologist.* I see normal-looking women, even women I admire, women with black hair to their waists, coming in and out of that door. It occurs to me that my school has made it easy to go to a shrink. It is something to do between classes, a way to shed worries before the next bell rings. I don't have to call anyone out there in Manhattan. I can just go to Chaucer class, eat my raisins, and stop briefly to have my head examined.

I descend to the office and knock. A small, elderly woman named, unbelievably, Dr. Grothe, cracks the door so I cannot see her patient. I tell her I would like to talk, and she says she can see me Thursday at ten. *I cannot step into her office that moment?* No, I have to have an appointment. How can I explain that my feelings are like robbers who must be caught while trashing the place? By Thursday, they may be still, back in a closet hidden by raisins and cheese and D. H. Lawrence. But I say nothing. I will see her Thursday.

On Thursday, I almost cancel. I do not want to offer the sight I have of my own life, the seconds that line themselves along my railing like cats to be fed. But I keep the appointment, climbing down the railed stairs that belong to early New York. This time Dr. Grothe's door is open. She is ready for me. I sit down and wait for her to begin. She does not speak. My voice cracks into the silence. I tell her that whatever was bothering me is gone. I laugh. She doesn't. *Why did I come?* She continues to look at me. She is beautiful, with white hair, a face thinned by age, and blue eyes, holding my worth in their gaze. *How did you feel on Monday?* What I expect as I answer her is that she is going to kick me out. I am a travesty to those who really need help. I am a pretender, a Camille. *Wipe your chin and get out.* But she leans forward and listens. My words are apologies, corrections, shame. She looks at her watch. *Next Thursday at ten?*

The subject, of course, is identity. Who am I without Deane? Do I exist without Deane? Will I kill Deane with my differences? We don't talk about this all at once, nor do I even recognize for a long time it is Deane we are talking about. I think we are talking about fear and anger and depression, about self-hatred and sorrow, about men and bodies, parents and childhood. But all along we are talking about Deane and how to live without her.

In her book, *Twins: Nature's Amazing Mystery*, author Kay Cassill, herself an identical twin, talks about "an urgency that all twins feel to be recognized as distinct personalities." Yet in my sessions with Dr. Grothe, the first of many therapists to work with me on my separation from Deane, she helped me understand how dangerous that urgency feels. For inherent in differentiation is competition, comparison, and departure, all treacherous for twins—so dependent on each other and sameness. I didn't want Deane to be better than me because then she would leave me. And for me to be better—read "different"—than Deane was subversive, mean, two-faced. To be disloyal is to have two faces, not one.

Life doesn't quite happen to a twin without her twin as witness. No event or feeling was quite real until the other entered it. "We" is the comfortable pronoun for twins, not "I." In fact, according to Cassill, twins have more trouble using pronouns than singletons, something I remember a teacher teasing me about.

"Why do you always talk in the first person plural?" she asked me, smiling like she'd caught me out. And she had: I felt ashamed, my dependence on Deane exposed.

In those hours with my therapist, I talk about the intensity of my desire to be with Deane. My craving for her is physical; I want to merge with her: I can't get close enough. And in that need is also sorrow. Because as the drive to be separate grows stronger, our ability to merge, to step inside each other's minds, grows less. So being with Deane becomes increasingly fraught. We fight because we cannot lose ourselves in each other as we once had. And unable to do that, we feel raw, exposed, and lonely. I don't want to be with other people who can never measure up to Deane, but I can no longer feel complete with Deane. I am both frustrated by our physical separation and bewildered as a newborn navigating a singleton world without her.

Inherent conflict has always been at the heart of twin mythology. Some American Indian tribes thought the first-born twin was a child of the Sun, the second the child of waters under the earth, representing evil. To Southwestern Indians, twins represented universal dualities: the sun and moon, light and dark, male and female, earth and sky. One without the other equaled imbalance, the universe off-kilter.

I understand imbalance. Without Deane, I lose half of my social repertoire. It has always been my role to make friends, but Deane's to keep them. I'm not good at keeping them because I have a quick tongue and temper. Deane's job is to sooth roughed-up feelings. I don't know how to do that.

In some hard-pressed African cultures, twins represented an economic threat, a blow to the harvest. In others, they portrayed infidelity. In more prosperous societies, twins were applauded, sometimes deified. But in others they were symbols of fertility: some cultures assigned twins to watch the flocks so the sheep would multiply. Others housed twins near water so the springs would be full of fish. The twin saints Cosmas and Damian are the patron saints of fertility. This rings true: surely part of my father's pride came from our visual display of *his* potency.

Twins are, of course, a simple fact of biology. A sperm fertilizes an egg, which then splits in two, each carrying the exact same genetic code: identical, or monozygotic twins. Fraternal, or dizygotic twins are something else: the fertilization of two eggs by two sperm. Although fraternal twins share some genes, the chances that all match are one in 200,000 trillion. So *twin* isn't truly the right word for fraternal births; they are siblings born at the same time. They are not, as Deane and I were, halves of the same matter.

Halves of the same matter, yes. But as I worked my way through my sessions with Dr. Grothe, I realized how much I longed to find out finally who I was without Deane. Her uncertainties about her own identity made mine seem only larger. As painful as it was to leave her and my parents, I was excited about it too, and Deane began to represent a drag on my longed-for independence. I felt furious at her for hanging on to me, and furious at myself for needing her. And if I left her, what would happen? Would she be the twin left behind and buried at the roadside? To leave her, I would harden my heart, and she would not forgive me. And then she would die.

Chapter 26

After the funeral, Dan and I drive from Philadelphia to Boston in Deane's car to pack her things. In front of the house is her garden—tomatoes, peppers, marigolds, basil. She would not spend another summer without one, she had told me.

"I don't want to be someone too busy for a garden."

So that summer she'd grown enough vegetables and herbs to make soups, enough flowers to fill vases. When she ran in the mornings through the cramped Somerville neighborhoods, she saw tiny front yards that her Italian neighbors filled with plants. Zucchini and eggplant hung from iron fences. Morning glories bloomed. But by the time she returned from her run, it was eight o'clock, and there was her thesis, a garden itself, and her patients in Chelmsford, and the squeeze of stress. Until one day at Star Market, they appeared: flats of seedlings. By dinnertime she had a garden next to her front porch. Her thesis wasn't done but her summer would blossom.

At the door, the names of her roommates are written in script below a detailed sketch of a flower. Deane's name is listed twice—her married name and above that Deane Foltz, the "Foltz" underlined. Dan and I climb the porch stairs to her apartment, where her roommates greet us and let us go alone to her room. The August heat has collected in the closed room, flays us as we go in. The open suitcase packed for Tennessee is on her bed. On her nightstand sit HiHo Crackers and Wilkie Collins's *The Moonstone*.

Drawer by drawer, hanger by hanger, I learn again what I had known and not known: her mix of logic and whimsy, of determined order and mess. Underwear mixed with extra film; socks with picture frames. A two-inch-high clay man whose hand holds tiny dried flowers. Tax records, boxed and dated. Candy and safety pins mixed in a jar.

I haul Deane's other suitcases out of her attic space, pile boxes on her bed. I find a pair of jogging pants I've given her, unworn. I want to get her something else. I keep on, sorting nothing because I want it all. I do not empty the ashtray in her car. How little she has: a bed, a basket, a rug, bookcases. Her bureau is borrowed, and tomorrow we will drive it back to its owner, easy duties.

I go down to the kitchen and in the cookbook stand find *The Vegetarian Epicure*, its pages opened to zucchini soup. The week before she died, Deane made five soups, had friends over to eat them. I pull her books from the shelf. At the top of many recipes she has written the date and a note. Deane's roommates have set her pots and bowls in the center of the kitchen, and I wrap them. The kitchen seems chaotic, out of sorts as if everyone is moving out.

The doorbell rings. It's Deane's former husband, Art. He has come to get her skis, skis he gave her. I pause on the stairway.

"For her?" I ask him. I turn my head toward the small dark-haired woman I see sitting in his truck.

I finish Deane's life, read her book, knit her sweater, carry her fury.

Even in my sorrow or perhaps because of it, I have plenty of room to be angry with Art for bringing a woman with him, for asking to keep the skis he gave her. It is irrational: he is still Deane's husband. But I am still angry at the hurt he caused my sister, angry because there is plenty to be mad at. Why not Art?

I think back to a summer night in Ann Arbor. The four of us are standing in an ice cream store, and Deane has ordered a cone.

"She doesn't need that," Art whispers to me.

I don't answer him, but I hurt for Deane. She has gained weight. She is too plump next to his wiry frame. He represses her zaftig exuberance.

His is Puritan stock. Arkansas is not good enough. One Thanksgiving, Deane and Art ask Dan and me to join them at Art's mother's house in Milton, Massachusetts, a starched enclave of privilege an hour or so from Boston. His mother's centuries-old house has bare wood floors and a lowered thermostat. The table has no gravy. We sit almost silent, the nephew—a boy—as formal as a diplomat.

"Yes, school is going quite well, thank you," he says. "And how are you?

Deane and I exchange glances, the boy robotic.

Later we play Scrabble as clinically as a set of interns arranging a cadaver. Dan and I are aching to leave.

But Deane found a way to love Art's mother, to admire her ability to raise her children alone. She was still able to offer her warmth, to see in her the best of what she loved in Art, even as she began to understand and assess her own unhappy marriage.

As I clear Deane's apartment, I also do the mundane. I go through her wallet for receipts. Dan and I go to her dry cleaners, thinking she may have left something there. The woman doesn't believe us, that Deane is dead. I stand in the cleaner's trying to persuade the woman that my sister is dead and I must have her clothes. I do not want to argue my sister's death. And then it doesn't matter. Let the cleaner keep the clothes. Except I want them. I want to know what they are, what she left and when.

This is the amazing thing about death: the living world knows nothing about it. The bills keep coming, the bank statements, even the phone calls. The Mary Kay salesperson calling for another order. The magazine renewals. The check-up reminders. This is when I begin to live the word *deceased. Write me a letter saying that your sister is deceased. Close the deceased's accounts. What is the deceased's full name?* The word is wrong. My sister is not deceased. She is robbed. Missing. Kidnapped. Murdered. Disappeared.

The language of death: deceased, internment, survivors.

The next day we return to the apartment for the last few things and for Deane's cat. Her roommates have set a ficus tree in the middle of her now empty room. It makes the room seem emptier, a shrine announcing my sister's absence, an announcement that nauseates me. I rush downstairs and sit on the porch steps. One of Deane's roommates follows me, puts her hand on my shoulder. I want to bite it. I want to say, *Why are you alive?* But my insides are locked up. I am polite, if speechless. I hate the permission for intrusion that loss brings. I can't control who knows, who gets to see me inside out. I want command over this death like a film-maker over each frame. I get to turn the film back. I get to be in front of the bullet. I get to knock Palmer down. I get to shut her roommate's mouth, who knows details I don't know, who makes me sick.

I go back upstairs to find the cat hiding under a broken floorboard in the attic. Mitty is broad as a beaver and neurotic as Woody Allen. She is cross-eyed, sweet, and maladjusted, a cat that slithered into hiding whenever Deane's lap was unavailable. Now she has slipped away from us just as we are ready to leave, Dan in the van and I in Deane's Volkswagen. We find a hammer and take up the floorboard, shine a light into that black space. No cat. Dan tries the dark, wet basement, moving to the far corner where mildewed mattresses lean against a wall, and behind them her eyes glow. Dan swoops her up and puts her in a traveling case in Deane's car, the car I'll drive while Dan mans the van.

As we drive, Mitty's meow turns into a low wail, a wail I feel free to join in, a wail we sing all the way to Virginia. I believe in the cat's grief. On the long stretches of highway I scream until my voice is hoarse, a pleasure after all these days of civilization. I can leave the windows closed and beat my fists on the steering wheel and let tears drip from my chin. But after a while, my throat hurts and I'm tired and I stop and watch the mountains start.

At a motel, we take the cat inside and set up her bowl and litter and hope for cover. We order a pizza and lie on the bed, staring at the TV. I am no company for Dan. I come in and out like light through smoky air. The television excuses us, offers a place to breathe, a place for Dan to rest from my grief. It is a relief now to go numb, to become charmless and unsmiling, to see no one who knows our heads are filled with death. We pour scotch and sodas, and rest the glasses on our breastbones. I am glad to be back in Appalachia, where I feel safe, where few people even know I am a twin. By now Danny is silent. He is Appalachian in his quiet, as are the still green forests we pass through and the blue glazed mountains. All night he is beside me, actual, as if I can't fall past him.

Chapter 27

Dan and I arrive in Knoxville and remember that our house has had no front door for three weeks. But nothing's changed. Here the clocks stopped. The pretend door is still propped in place, leaning. On the kitchen table lies the Ph.D. gift—a belt—its card addressed to Dr. Deane. In the refrigerator, the champagne. We bring in Mitty and introduce her to Snagglepuss, our cat. Years before, Deane and I had found the two kittens together at a farmers market. They are littermates, sisters rejoined. For weeks Mitty lives behind the refrigerator. I place a bowl of water and food beside it, but we never see her. Her sad withdrawal makes more sense to me than the world's insistence. I am the cat. I am behind my own refrigerator. She comes out at night as I do in my sleep.

Sleep becomes relief. That's where I meet Deane, where I get to back life up. In these dreams, Deane's hair is short and curly, growing out of the gunshot. I crawl through an attic looking for her and she sits in the corner, waiting. Or she is sick and I get to say goodbye. But some dreams are filled with panic. I come home to my parents for the summer only to find out Deane has died or will die, and I can't change it. Death is the new unstoppable fact. In my dreams, I slow it down, I control it. Deane and I work out a deferred separation. She will know what is happening to me, she will sanction it. I want her to know my sorrow because only she can know it.

Mornings after she died, I open my eyes and I am mindless, the world unchanged: a blue sky, a bright sun, a bird at the window, a day to rush into. And then, the world with a piece out. Which was it—the bright sun or the one thing that could not be true?

Waking is the moment I shrink from. Because waking, I have forgotten. The world is as it was. And in the same instant, I remember. I wake up, and the light is a wall I can't budge, a house surrounded by vines that grow in the window, down the chimney, through the pipes. All day I go through that Friday. I am James Palmer sitting in the parking lot waiting for Deane to arrive. I am Deane climbing out of the car in my mauve silk shirt, the world light, my thesis at the typist, the air beginning to smell of autumn. I am Deane rising from my swivel chair when Palmer bursts into my office. I see him, and I see his gun, and I know that I am going to die. And then I start the film again. I persuade Deane to visit me the day before—as we had talked about. I go to Lowell and smash my body into Palmer's. I go there and part of the bullet comes through me.

Mornings, I get up and drive with Danny to his work. He drops me at the library, and I carry in a box of Deane's papers. I sit facing the window where no one can see me. I read the notes she wrote as a student teacher. I read her letters of application to graduate school, and I read the correspondence with her thesis advisors. I read her promise to read more and work harder. Some papers—duplicates, forms—I throw away. Others I send to my parents or Deane's friends. For four hours I sort and file.

I read her diaries, her senior year in high school first. "You two really love each other, don't you?" the gym teacher said to her one day, watching the two of us joke and talk in gym. I'm struck by how much she writes about her boyfriend Bill. He is the instrument of our separation, the spread of her love from me to him. And yet, whatever good happens for me, happens to her. She is thrilled that I like Scott, happy when I win a radio contest, reprimanding when she thinks I have been unkind to a boy who likes me. I see we are separating but not quite. Sometimes, she comes over from her room to spend the night in mine, like a sleepover that makes her happy. She writes about how much work she has, how hard she studies, and a mist of anxiety hovers over the diary. She is too fat, too lonely, too tired, too scared of not doing well. I read the Foltz lines everywhere: the inheritance from our father of worry and fear. How can we be good enough? That is always his question and ours.

I go into the library bathroom, where I can make noise as I cry, and the bathroom soap smells like the hospital. When I meet Danny for lunch, he sees that my eyes are red. He knows that I cried all morning. But we talk about the soup, about his teaching, about what we will have for dinner that night.

At home, I sort Deane's clothes. I hang two ropes across the guest bedroom and turn it into a closet, a display room sloppy as a discount store. Each day, I pick out something new to wear, to try on, to see if it can become as much me as Deane. But most of the clothes are pure Deane, and I am an imposter. She loved maroons and mauves, floral prints, and silks, cowl neck sweaters, a high degree of femininity. And she had the closet of a pro: jackets and heels that somehow she pulled off without looking stiff as a congresswoman. Her clothes always had flow. The imperceptible creep of difference began when we split up and lived apart, our personalities now easier to separate. Deane's clothes became more muted, as she was, more quiet and feminine. Mine were, like me, a bit bolder, a bit angrier—a red sweater with lightning stripes.

I wear things once and then decide, Goodwill or my closet. I keep pieces I gave her and those that remind me of her: her red cashmere sweater, her jeans, her kelly green sweatshirt. The florals are tossed, the padded jackets, the silks flutter onto the giveaway pile.

In Deane's clothes I feel close to her. I am always wondering what she knows. It is my new job to wonder. I sit in the library trying to write poetry, but the poems are all about Deane. I use words to hunt a hidden landscape, creating a place where she might be and then erasing it.

One more time,
Your hand, small as a wren
Falls off the bed.
I lift it,
Our shuttle to a sagging sky.

On days I don't meet Dan for lunch, I sit outside in the grass. Around me, the trees blaze. The sky has never held such depth, such distance. I want the world to unlock itself.

I lose twenty pounds. I cannot concentrate on hunger. I take a few bites, and then I remember and my stomach heaves and lunch is over. But I like being skinny. I have never been this thin. I am disappearing or making myself small enough to disappear. I am making myself unlike Deane. Her clothes swim on me, and I take them to a seamstress. "My, you've lost weight," she says. I stand still, letting her stickpins into the waistband. I look in the mirror. I sit at my dressing table and look at my bony face, putting on Deane's makeup, covering my dark circles. At first all I see is Deane. When I see her in the mirror looking back, I start to cry, and she cries with me. But as I lose weight I see something else: this new face, my own face of sorrow. I will never again look like Dorothy. I will never again look like Deane. Her face is gone and so is mine.

Chapter 28

When Deane and I part at age nineteen, we shed the confusion that has followed us all our lives. In a new life, people don't know we are twins. People use my name with confidence. They don't compare me to Deane or ask me to deliver a message to her. They don't grin and say, "Now you are? . . ." Being one of a kind feels simple, relaxing. No explanations. No eany, meany, mo. Except we have internalized the confusion. I am not quite sure who I am without Deane, nor she without me. I travel by train on weekends to visit her in Philadelphia. As I walk from 30th Street Station, we see each other and start to run. From the moment we are together, we are happy. We make plans: we'll go out to dinner, we'll go shopping, we'll do homework. The next day we walk the Philadelphia streets, popping into every store. Everything feels possible. I find a bright red sweater with black zigzags and Deane juts her thumbs up. For forty bucks, I am reinvented.

Still, this living apart isn't easy. Separation is a seesaw of ambivalence: sorrow weights one end, exhilaration the other. People think I am just like them, but I have this secret: someone else in the world looks just like me.

In the end we want each other's company more than independence. We decide to live together for the summer. We sign up for classes—different ones—at Harvard, find an apartment in Cambridge, one we share with a pretty woman named Louise. Soon Louise has a boyfriend, Fritz, and the four of us sit around like two couples, eating junk food and watching TV. Deane and I, for most people, come together like married people. We're shared. If you tell one of us something, you feel you've told both of us. If one's invited, we both are. We don't set the rules; that's just the way it works.

Louise is unhappy too, at odds about her future as a doctor, and our antics cheer or distract her. Her angst is loneliness, but we show her something else: that love and intimacy are complicated and tangled. She watches our friendship, and she's fascinated and frightened. Who wouldn't laugh seeing two people who look just alike? Who doesn't want an alter ego? And yet the squirmy reality of *I* is tough enough without the blur of identical faces and bodies, without the constant question: Who is who?

That summer, Deane and I meet every day after class. That summer, men land on the moon and Ted Kennedy plunges into a creek, and we discover being together no longer makes us happy. In our tiny apartment, we bake bread, and while it rises, we sit feeling puffy in the living room, watching the world through the TV screen.

We want something more than we can offer each other, grabbing for some dim answer to our anxiety on the lip of the world. We fight, and always underneath the fight is the wish that we could soothe each other.

"Aren't you going to eat that?" Deane points to my half sandwich.

"I'm not hungry."

"I hate you. I know you're not eating just to show off."

I can see she's going to pinch me. I like being thinner than she is. I smirk about it. I am unkind in my victory, and that gets her crazy. Or this:

"Why can't you go?" I ask Deane.

"Because I have too much work to do."

"What work?"

She's not looking at me now.

"I hate you. You're always working. I'm going alone."

"Go alone."

I stay home and study.

I work at being wilder than Deane, moving toward riskier boys than Deane. I push away by being the daring one, the one who hitchhikes and writes poetry, who drinks wine at poetry parties, who is drawn to risky people. Deane doesn't like it. My bravado makes her feel boring, but she is also comfortable in her sanity, her old-fashioned attachments to the Supremes and the Righteous Brothers. She is drawn to people who work hard, to people who activate in a crisis instead of ruminating solutions. She is furious with my yen for crazy, perhaps because she knows at heart it isn't me or because it leaves her behind. Or because she is afraid of the people I bring home, that I could get hurt. One guy makes copies at a copy store: the next moment he is kissing me on my bed. I am scared, but I want to be that risk taker, if only to make certain I'm not Deane. I take to wearing my hair up, to wearing bare-shouldered dresses, to acting far more mysterious with strangers than I feel. Deane is reasoned. She has plans. She wants to make money. I want to be Sylvia Plath or Carson McCullers. I want to wear weird clothes and live in the Village. If I wear black tights and short skirts and take up with strangers and join a women's co-op and send poems off to magazines and smoke dope with boyfriends I hardly know, won't that sever me from Deane, announce I am distinct?

"You don't have to be so crazy," she says. "It's not good for you."

"You don't have to tell me what to do."

"I don't want you here when you're like this."

"Like what?"

"Like you don't care."

We sit on the sofa after school, eating wedges of cheese and home-made bread, hating each other and ourselves, wishing we could go home.

"Just don't make friends with everyone in every store we go in, okay?"

"I embarrass you."

"You do. It's embarrassing."

"Okay."

Apart, we feel uncertain, unformed. Together, two girls rolled off a mimeo, we fight. Maybe one of us will pull ahead, leave the other behind. Be less available. Stop reading her mind.

The summer we graduate from college, we move again to Cambridge. We take a publishing course and share an apartment. But I have a boyfriend who keeps telling me I have to leave Deane. When I'm with her, we fight. And childhood hovers like a dense fog. I keep looking over my shoulder for my parents. I can't be new because Deane sees my fear and I hers. When we are alone in the apartment, it feels scary, the way it feels being home alone as children. We are at the edge of adulthood looking out over some kind of chasm we're certain to fall into. I sit in my anxiety and in hers, the dose doubled, and neither of us can stand it.

"Do you think I look fat today?"

"Don't ask me that."

"What's wrong with you?"

"Have you finished the assignment? Can I see it?"

"You need some mascara."

"Well."

"What?"

"Well, who else is going to tell you?"

"Well, who asked you?"

I move out ostensibly to live with my boyfriend, but it is really my attempt to outrun anxiety. I have picked a man I do not love but one I feel safe with. I met him in Chock Full of Nuts on Broadway in New York. He stared at me, his bright blue eyes behind rimless spectacles that give him a John Lennon look. He has a thick shag of gray-blond hair and a thin, wiry body. He is not my type; what I am drawn to is his fascination with me. That I could attract such a radical-looking man—a former student of the German philosopher Herbert Marcuse—surprised me. I am no Yoko Ono. But he is fascinated by my twinness and fantasizes about being with both of us. When I leave New York, he does too, renting an apartment in Cambridge, where he spends days working on his doctoral thesis on the philosopher Jean-Jacques Rousseau. He quizzes me about what being a twin is like. *Do you feel what she feels? Do you know which one you are?* He is a tuning fork to the hum of my confusion. He divines what others do not: that I am fighting to pull from my sister; that I am used to traveling two by two. He is willing to be my second.

I move in with him because I have nowhere else to go. That lasts less than a week. His intensity scares me. His dreams of twins scare me. His willingness to merge is exactly what I want and exactly too dangerous.

But Stephen only asks what everyone wants to ask: *Just how connected, how identical are you? Do you have extrasensory perception?* The subtext: *Are you as freaky as you appear?* The answer is both simple and complicated. No, we do not have extrasensory perception. No, I do not know what is happening to Deane when we are apart. But no relationship compares to the one between twins. We began as one cell. We had our own language. No one, unpracticed, can tell us apart.

As girls, we imagine our life in the womb. We are having a great time of it, laughing, talking, sharing secrets, commenting on the dining services, arguing over who got the greater share. We decide that my two curved fingers and spine are the results of fights we had over birth, over who should go first. I imagine Deane thrusting her shoulder at mine, shoving as I refuse to budge, furious that I will have to fight my way out while she lounges, waiting for her chance to swagger on through.

In this fantasy, we give nothing to our mother; birth has nothing to do with her body, with when she is ready for labor, and everything to do with our readiness to leave the cozy womb. We already see life as our collaboration: if Deane was getting enough to eat, I probably was too. If she thought the womb too crowded, then I could feel the pinch as well.

I read of country singers, the Louvin Brothers, brothers whose voices twinned in harmony. Then one brother, Ira, died in a car accident. Charlie continued solo for five decades.

"But when it comes time for the harmonies to come in, I still move to my left to give the harmony room," Charlie says, "knowing that there's no harmony standing on my right."

This is how I feel: I still move to my left.

After I leave Stephen, I try an apartment with roommates I've never met. They're gum-snapping toughs. I stuff my things into a cab and go back to Deane's. By then she has found another roommate, but she lets me sleep in her room. She welcomes me back by cooking for me—fried chicken, cornpone, graham cracker brownies—as our mother would. We're healthy enough to know we don't want to be the two old ladies who never marry, who dress alike, who live together. And yet we also know that we already are those ladies.

At the end of summer, we both get new apartments, new roommates. I live on the other side of Cambridge, and on Sundays I hop in a cab and for a dollar ride to Deane's apartment. I buy a bicycle so I can bike over. I get a job as a receptionist at the Radcliffe Admissions Office, and Deane works as a secretary at the *Harvard Crimson*. We meet for breakfast or lunch in Harvard Square, eating slices of bread and cheese we bring from home. One day we walk toward each other and realize we are wearing the same dress, yellow prints our mother sent us. We each duck behind a tree. *Not today,* we call to each other.

I like having my own life, but I am lonely. I walk to work each morning, and one day Deane sees me as she passes by in a bus.

"I felt like Dr. Zhivago," she says, remembering the scene in the 1965 movie by that name in which Zhivago, separated for years from his love Lara, sees her from a bus and, frantic to reach her, has a heart attack and dies. The surprise that one of us could exist independently is childlike, the same surprise a first grader feels passing her teacher far from school. We are developmentally delayed. We are not quite sure how to function. Like the newly divorced or widowed, we begin by going through the motions.

At an apartment gathering my roommate has, I meet a radical-like graduate student with a head full of curly hair and a face of delicate features. He invites me to dinner, and I spend the night. I think I am falling in love. He comes up behind me as I stand by his window and kisses my neck. I am so ready to be his, to ease away from my sister into another intimacy, to trade ours for an intimacy that doesn't show, that's not quite so public.

I comb Cambridge for a willing proxy. I join a women's group and take a poetry class. I dream of my parents' house and long to go home, not as I am now, but as a child. I do not want this grown-up life without Deane.

Deane, meanwhile, is channeling her angers into her secretarial job at the *Harvard Crimson*. She writes an editorial that begins, "I cannot be Batman to every Robin," referring to fledgling reporters who show up, blaming her for their misplaced copy. "What I criticize is a world that makes it acceptable to say to a secretary, 'Be a sweet girl and give me a pen so I can finish writing my feature about the oppression of people in Vietnam.'"

She is much more invested in her job than I am, going in on Saturdays to finish her work, staying there late during the week. She has a drive, a seriousness that impresses me, but that I don't quite understand.

"Why would you go in after hours?" I ask her.

"I have work," she shrugs.

"You're the secretary."

I see I'm going to piss her off. She is short-tempered these days. She's mad at the world. She's mad at what stops her. It is, easily, the worst year of my life so far. I live with a roommate who is diabetic and suicidal, another who is recovering from an abortion, and a third whose optimism heals us all. I hate my job of answering phones and filing letters. The days drip by. At noon, on the days I don't meet Deane, I climb the stairs of the white-frame house where I work to make my lunch, a smear of peanut butter on white. When no one is in the office, I read *Ethan Frome*. I long to plunge into the snow. I think about the women in their fifties who work in the university basement from eight to five and wonder if I too will file away my life underground.

I earn $90 a week. I begin to dream of becoming a dancer, of going to graduate school in writing. I begin to dream about leaving my sister. I apply for graduate school at the University of Chicago, and Deane applies to the Eliot Pearson School of Child Study at Tufts. This calms her. I have a therapist who has pointed out that my life cannot begin until I separate from Deane, and I believe her. I dream of Chicago, of going where no one knows me. My plans to depart scare my sister. She can feel me floating away. But to feel our separation would stop me, and so I do not feel. I send away for applications, I file them, and then I wait for spring.

Chapter 29

I am not the only one to flounder. Without Deane, the places in our family shift. My parents see me as a conduit to Deane, and I can only fail them. They come to visit and my mother gets off the plane and begins to cry when she sees me.

"I wish it had been me instead of Deane," she sobs, enfolding me.

She has been drinking, and her voice carries through the quiet, Knoxville airport. I want to hustle her out, muffle her crying. Her tears won't stop.

Her sadness upsets my father, and she begins to hide it from him. She sits in the tiny family room and works crossword puzzles and watches game shows, and drinks. She drinks quietly so no one sees her, but her attention slurs. Workmen arrive, and she is folded sideways on the sofa. We know but we say nothing. She drinks before she goes to play golf in the mornings, and the women whisper that it's understandable, her daughter shot in the head. Her friends begin to treat her tentatively, gingerly, like she is ill, and she is.

She goes to the dermatologist to have a cancerous spot removed from her nose. While my father waits for her in the waiting room, he finds an empty vodka miniature in her purse.

This covert drinker is not the mother I remember from my childhood, but now I am uncertain. What amber mixed with her Coca-Cola? She was for us the warm place on the sofa, the pillow for TV. On days we watched movies together, I climbed behind her, sitting on the sofa neck, brushing her hair over and over. But now I realize that she had no one, no one she trusted. Whatever fears she had she kept apart, and when we left for school, she had long days without us, days when it would have been easy to pour one drink and then another.

My father spends more time at home, he arranges for the cleaning lady to be there when he's not. He calls me, and I hear his voice roughen.

He works on my sister's estate, complicated because she died the week her divorce was to be final. Deane's husband, Art, hires a lawyer, as does my father. (Art gets the house; we get the death benefit.) My father immerses himself in legal arguments, riding to the Philadelphia law office, faxing updates to my brother and me. He takes care of Deane by unraveling legalities, by activity—as I do. He buys a dogwood tree and plants it in her name at the church. He keeps fresh flowers on her grave. On nice days, he walks the mile from home to the gravesite.

As my mother's grief turns inward, she pulls my father to her. Within a year of my sister's death, she is his full-time job. He takes her to a party, and she falls in the icy driveway. My dad helps her up. Her hose is torn, her skirt smeared with snow and gravel.

"Take me home," she says.

"Are you okay?" he says.

"Get me to the car."

For a while they ride in silence.

"Deanie, you have to stop drinking," says my father.

"Leave me alone."

"I can't have it."

When they get home, she goes into the guest room bathroom, the place Dad lets her smoke. She inhales her cigarette, finishes her drink. When she goes into their bedroom, the lights are out. She gets into her twin bed alone.

They both come to visit me, and she falls asleep at the dinner table. I have made a special dinner: pasta primavera. I look across the table, and my beautiful mother's chin rests on her chest, her eyes closed. She slumps to the side in the chair. When my father leaves the room, she wakes up and asks me to fix her a drink.

"Mom, I can't," I say as softly as I can.

"Before he gets back," she says.

"I can't."

Behind her glasses, her eyes are angry. She wraps her arms around her body and sits up straight, turns her face away from me, gives me the stiff shoulder, the silent fury announcing the end of speech for several days. She is not mad that I don't get her a drink; she will find her way there. It's what I imply: that she is her father, that she is a drunk, that I am in league with Dad, and damn us all.

In another year, my father and my mother's sister place her in an alcohol treatment center for six weeks where no family is allowed to speak to her. She is furious, but she goes. I sit at home on my bright yellow couch trying to imagine her as she moves among the other women, her stiff reserve, her denial that she is like them. Dad says her days are full of activities—cards, bingo, walking, counseling. I imagine her talking to a shrink. She is the patient who says as little as possible, the polite Southern lady. She'll talk about the weather, her children, ask the doctor about his children, when she can go home. Only, I wish speech for her, that she can finally talk about how scared she is, that she married the wrong man, that she can ask, *Is it too late for me?*

After a month, the doctor lets Dad take her to lunch. She chooses Howard Johnson's so that she can eat a fried clam roll with a Coca-Cola—a place my white tablecloth Dad would never go. She seems so small in the world, so HoJo, so little she wants. But they have a good time, they laugh. She orders a second Coke. She asks about me, about Jeff. She asks when she can come home. He drives her back to the facility. I imagine she is not unhappy to step out of the car, these weeks the longest she has ever been away from either her mother or husband, no one bossing her, criticizing. She hardly knows who she is, and she can hardly find out fast enough.

When she calls me at the end of her treatment, her first question is *How is your writing?*—a question she's not asked for years. I love the steady ladder of her voice. My mother back. I answer briefly, tentatively, blandly.

"It's fine."

"What are you working on?"

"A long poem, a narrative."

"I want to see."

"I want you to."

I had not realized how far away grief and alcohol had taken her. My mother had become an angry, paranoid woman, and I had buried the other one. In her voice, I hear all the first-grade afternoons she welcomed me home in her big embrace, the ways she stooped down so that she could put one arm around me and one around Deane, then stand up and take our hands to go home.

She was, of course, still far away. She never once told me directly where she had been or any details about it. Dad went and picked her up, and again they stopped for clam rolls, a date with Cokes. Two weeks later Dad found two unopened bottles of cooking sherry in the car.

"Deanie, what are you doing?" he asked her, carrying them into the kitchen.

"I didn't drink them."

That was all the liquor he found or saw. But her hands still shook, and her walk was unsteady. When she made dinner, she leaned her elbows on the counter to prop herself up.

There is to her now only ill sorrow. With my father, she is silent because he has asked her to be. She sits in the den filling out a crossword puzzle, and when she calls me, she has little to say, as if she simply wants to hear me breathing on the phone to reassure herself our connection is still alive. What I know now is that her diminishment shouldn't have happened. The strange intersection of her fragile father, her demanding mother, echoes in her marriage. And the young, beautiful girl, the young queen at her May Day Ball, disappeared, the only feedback the sad scary thoughts planted in her childhood that the world is peopled with violent villains. What her childhood predicted, what she waited for, came true: she had a terrifying vindication of her certainties in my sister's death and in her own illness. I watched her slip away, guessing part of her was glad.

Chapter 30

I walk along Cambridge streets, waiting for an envelope to change my life. My reach toward the future consoles me. I have applied for a change, and so until I hear something, I breathe. I am no longer marching in place. Before me is the wall of my future, and I have etched in a door.

When I am accepted into a writing program at the University of Chicago, my therapist is delighted and Deane despondent. More than despondent. Furious. Furious that I am abandoning her, that I am leaving her in a two-room apartment with a depressed roommate and her own fear. She was accepted at Eliot-Pearson, and no wonder. In her application essay, she talks about the mute girl she taught as a camp counselor who, by the end of the summer, would whisper to her. She talks about her work with disturbed adolescents at the Home for Little Wanderers, how much more she could have done with training.

"What frustrated me most was sensing so intensely the needs of these young people and realizing that in spite of good intentions and determination, without training I was powerless to help them. I want to learn, and I ask you to help me . . .

"In part, we are forever what our backgrounds have made us. But I am young enough to believe too that we become what we dream. . . . I am eager, and I am impatient to start."

Somehow as we both make these next choices, they feel combative, chin-jutting. *I will too go to graduate school. I will too keep going.* I am too scared about my own choice to consider Deane's, and she knows that. She is furious with my blindness, my habit of wearing blinders, seeing only what I can handle, not what is there. So, even before I leave her, I have left her. What she doesn't know is how good a choice she's made, that she is leaving me just as I am leaving her.

My twin-obsessed ex-boyfriend introduces me to Cathy, another identical twin he is dating who is going to the University of Chicago. She is tall, skinny, talkative, with a big laugh and a penchant for Mexican embroidered clothing and big earrings. I like her. We spend an evening drinking red wine and listening to Anne Sexton read poetry beside the Charles, and we decide to live together in Chicago.

When the movers don't come on time, I leave my boxes with Deane and climb into a car with another twin and drive across the country. I am buoyant with adventure.

In Chicago, Cathy and I move temporarily into an apartment with four men who are geology students and cavers. Most of the time, they are below ground on their bellies, surfacing only to gorge themselves at all-you-can-eat buffets and to set up their apartment rooms like substitute caves. Our favorite, John, wears a small searchlight band around his forehead, as if he anticipates a Chicago blackout. Or maybe he likes being at the ready to crawl back into the earth's womb. Whenever he peers into the packed refrigerator, his headlight circles the meat, the milk, the mayonnaise. Inside his cramped room, he has pitched a single-person tent where he sleeps. But amid his compulsion, down below the rocks and searchlights, lies John's humor, his mouth a slight curve as if he knows a laugh could pitch forward any second. He's great looking: a dark, wiry, short guy with snappy brown eyes, a shadow of beard on his face. But he's without conceit because his center lies in a cave; it's too dark for him to notice he's handsome.

Cathy and I sit at the kitchen table eating bread and orange cheese, smoking cigarettes, circling apartment ads. Our roommates rotate in and out during our lunch, benign and hungry. John sits down with us at the table, blocking the swing in the refrigerator door, spreading his hands on the newspaper to tell us which ads look good. He bolts two bologna sandwiches, swilling water from his canteen. Cathy and I star the places he says are safe, and in the afternoon we walk the steamy streets back and forth, looking for a place to live. Cathy walks as fast as she talks, almost dancing across the Chicago heat.

One day I head out by myself, taking a bus across town to a realty office. As the bus drifts farther from the campus, white passengers disappear, and I am the only white person on the bus, a source of curiosity. I find the realty and present an ad for the apartment I'd like to see. The realtor says it's taken, and I start to cry.

"But I called," I say.

The realtor, alarmed, leans toward me.

"Now, little lady, let me see if I can find you something."

I snuffle into a Kleenex. "I can't find anything."

"I imagine it's tough," says the realtor, "what with the little one on the way."

I nod, simultaneously encouraged and horrified. I am wearing a tent dress. That, combined with hormonal hysteria, surely equals pregnancy. I switch a ring I am wearing to my wedding finger. This could work in my favor.

"Right," I answer, crying a little harder now.

We drive together to a brick building, the man casting furtive looks my way, eyeing me gingerly as if I might disperse more display from my rounded tent. He shows me a small apartment, rough but freshly painted. But it is far from campus. I shake my head and accept his offer of a ride back across Woodlawn.

Later that afternoon, I hit the street alone again, soon walking behind a short, bald man with a huge ring of keys on his belt. I run to catch up with him.

"Do you know any apartments for rent?"

He stops and looks me up and down. "I have one. You a student?"

Yes, yes, a wonderful responsible clean paying student.

White and large and old, the apartment is beautiful. The landlord and his wife are from Czechoslovakia, and the floors are swept and shiny, the walls newly painted. The kitchen looks out on a tiny green lawn sprinkled with apple trees. Cathy and I put cushions on our black trunks, and they become sofas. Cathy decorates like she dresses, and soon everything has crisp modern colors, like she does. We opt for spare but bright, celebrate by inviting our cavers over for a spread, mounds of fried chicken and hot doughnuts we make ourselves, rolled in cinnamon sugar. The cavers love us; we can tell by the mounded bones. Our life has started.

I also begin the year by losing fifteen pounds, the belly baby. Cathy is even more weight obsessed than I am, although she is thinner. She turns eating into a competition. We will see who can eat the least. We set up the classic twins' rivalry, as if it were part of the house. Our symbiosis is the tube of oxygen we tug around the apartment so we can breathe. We learn to move in lockstep, to shop together, cook together, to share each other's clothes. At night, we lie on our stomachs on the living room floor and read the newspaper, sipping half glasses of Spanada or beer. With each other as shadow, we learn to be alone—or think we do. I practice living apart from Deane by finding her substitute.

Years later, I read in Kay Cassill's book *Twins* that it is not uncommon for twins—consciously or not—to seek out other twins. So much of the work is done already: without speaking, we know so much about each other that singletons do not. But Cathy isn't Deane. Being in lockstep with Cathy feels dangerous. I don't want to be so close, maybe because I know how to, and so does she. I want to be apart. Although I seek Deane everywhere, she is only of me, not apart. In John Donne's poem "Valediction Forbidding Mourning," he describes the separation of two lovers as "gold to airy thinness beat." Apart, Deane and I are not separate, our union a fine, thin fabric that binds us.

I don't know Cathy: we have known each other only months. In our friendship, I am the quiet one, a new role. Like any new friends, Cathy and I care what we think of each other. We look for thin ice. Thin ice doesn't exist between twins. Anger, jealousy, but not distance, or apathy, or misunderstanding. Deane's attention is empathetic: "profound understanding," says Cassill. Deane understands what I say and the white space of what I don't say. We are stems from the same root, split only above ground.

I slip into a man's white shirt and blue jeans and go to a football scrimmage. The cavers, in an uncharacteristic dip into fresh air, come along. I sit by the field and realize I am no longer fat; I am sexy. Is it sexy to be independent, to reinvent who I think I am? Oh yes. I don't even know that other Dorothy. I schedule an 11 o'clock class on Tolstoy, and I believe I am Sonya. I have taken a bad life locked in the stale offices of Radcliffe Admissions and flung open the doors to the midwestern prairies. I have crossed the plains in a covered wagon, and now I am a pioneer in Chicago, where no one knows me, and I am waiting for Levin to show up with his grains and his farm to marry me. I have never been happier. For once I am content to sit on the lip of my life.

Every day before class, I use the ladies' room on the second floor of Humanities, a building of stone that seems more like a cathedral than an academic hall. The bathroom is old with huge, rippled windows that open out, and when I lean over the ledge I can see the campus. In the bathroom is a full-length mirror. I bend over and brush my hair from the neck forward, then stand up to let it fall back on my shoulders. I look in the mirror, and I turn into a woman. One of those days I look in the mirror, and realize I am in love.

Larry showed up at my apartment door one evening in early November, dark, thin, balding, a former Columbia student looking for a Barnard girl. He is strikingly handsome, with high cheekbones and a rat-tat-tat laugh with a zipper grin. He's a former Columbia quarterback, and he moves like an athlete, his body taut and beautiful. In short, he puts a spell on me: I find him, his looks, his foreignness irresistible.

He invites me to a party where we dance in the dark, drink too much, kiss at the doorstep. But I don't know this person, Larry, who has to study all the time, who doesn't touch me except to kiss, who watches for me as I cross the campus. I attach myself to him the way other people commit to jobs or fat novels. Slipping inside someone's skin is what a twin does, and I do it beautifully and heedlessly. When we sit in the kitchen talking, I find him sometimes boring, the stories long or disjointed. What I want is the kissing, the romance, the fighting, and then the making up.

What does a twin find in her first real affair? I had moved to the middle of the United States, where the news does not originate in New York and people vacation on lakes, not oceans. I had moved to find a blankness I could impress, and I am having an affair with a man I can't talk to or spend time with. He is the ferryman taking me to myself through waters of narcissism and escape. I don't have time to think about friendship. When we aren't spending the night together, I read Tolstoy or sit in a dark theatre listening to my professor talk about Tolstoy. But instead of Levin coming to save me, it's Larry. In truth, he is saving no one.

The more obsessed I become with Larry, the less I depend on Deane, my far-away sister. When I go to see her that fall, my myopia maddens her. Larry is just another Deane proxy, an edifice that separates me from my old life but also from fear. I haven't learned independence; I've learned replacement, and Deane knows it.

"Can't you talk about something else besides Larry?" she snaps.

"I'm hungry."

"You're not eating."

"I want you to meet him. I am too."

"How could you not be hungry?"

She watches me with disgust as I eat cold Chinese vegetables. She hasn't met Larry. What she's met before is my impulsiveness. *Who is this person? Why aren't you here?*

Deane's still in her tiny apartment. She has started school and is full of anxiety and loneliness. She has found a psychiatrist who says her backache stems from depression, who talks to her of her fury at my independence, her longing to be home. He is her social life: her plunge into therapy is as distancing as my plunge into Chicago. When she seems detached, I know she is thinking about Dr. Free, wondering what he would say about this or that. When I mention her distraction, she laughs, embarrassed but without denial. She takes me with her for her appointment, drops me on a corner to shop, picks me up an hour later, more distracted than before.

"I'm mad at you for leaving me," she says.

"I know that," I say.

"You haven't really, have you?"

"Never. But yes."

Her grieving passes over me like bad weather. Larry is, after all, *my* fantasy. He is the prop I use to move into a new life. As I use him, I also begin to notice, almost to my irritation, that he is real. I notice because he begins to tell me things that scare me: how he had a breakdown in college, how he had a mental health deferment from the military. I visit him at his parents' home in New Jersey over Christmas vacation, and in their house he seems a silent shadow.

His parents are Jewish refugees who'd escaped Hitler and Austria in World War II and found their way to New Jersey. His older sister married and moved abroad, so Larry was left to tend parents who approach the world with anxiety, an anxiety that spilled like acid onto him.

"Why'd you buy that coat? It looks like *schmata*," says his father of Larry's pea coat, one we picked together. "You spent fifty dollars on that? We don't have it."

"Leave me alone," says Larry. "I like it. We're leaving."

"Where? When will you be back?"

"When we're back, Dad."

Embarrassed, I smile at his father, a short, balding man with white hair below his dome. I wander into their living room and look at the family pictures. In them Larry looks lost, sad, receding beside his animated sister. I feel a fear growing in my stomach, but I ignore it. *We are still possible,* I think.

When we leave at four in the morning to drive back to Chicago, I find cruising in the dark with the man I love wildly romantic. I savor the miles. I smoke cigarettes and drink coffee and watch the sun come up. We stop for cheese sandwiches, and I don't mind that Larry hasn't spoken in hours. I play both parts: his love, my love. Because I am still willing Tolstoy to write the story.

In February, Larry's roommates call to say that Larry has tried to kill himself and is in the hospital.

On the psychiatric ward, Larry sits in a blue-flowered gown, his eyes full of shame and fear, and I see him for the first time. He drove to the gas station–convenience store on his corner and bought a bottle of Drano and drank it like a bad cocktail. He slit his wrists with a razor and lay down on his bedsheets. The Drano burned his esophagus so that he cannot speak. His wrists are wrapped in white gauze like a player before a football game. I never find out who saved him.

Now he is on a locked ward where his mother sits, her English sliding back into German.

I go to Larry's apartment to clean his room, to clean what his mother shouldn't see. I gather bloody sheets. Larry moves back to New Jersey, and I cut my long hair, as if to say we can start over. The doctors say Larry has bipolar disorder, or manic depression. We met on the top of his ride. And then despite love and Tolstoy and Levin, Larry began to slide where nothing is possible. Sentences don't fit together, and love is nowhere on the map.

His face whitens. He shaves off his mustache, and he stays indoors. He takes thorazine, which keeps him sleepy and hungry. In Chicago, I continue the fantasy that we can return to our early romance, that he can be my sexy boyfriend. I don't want to give up on this passion, this handsome mystery I know nothing about. His angst only makes him more appealing—a brooding Heathcliff. So we continue our relationship, talking every day by phone. I am certain love will cure him; I refuse to believe our story can get uglier.

When I visit in the spring, we take a blanket to a park above the Hudson. Cuts in his wrists are pink under a fat leather watchband. He stares out at the water, his slow thick fog more than silence, my first sighting of gloom and terror, of what you can't leave behind. I begin to realize that he's not good for me, that I can't cure him, but I can't leave him either. He needs me, I think, and I am afraid he will kill himself if I call it quits. He is so scared.

"I'm not even sure I could be a shoe salesman," he tells me. He applies for that job but doesn't get it.

That May, Deane and a boyfriend Jack come to Chicago. On the spur of the moment, they suggest we drive to New York City, surprise Larry after his appointment with his psychologist, and drive to stay with Jack's friends in upstate New York for the weekend.

One glimpse of Larry skirting the Manhattan sidewalk tells us we made a dreadful mistake. He is pale and shaky. He climbs into the car, angry, unwelcoming.

"I can't handle this kind of surprise," he says to me, clearly shaken.

We travel to the beautiful farmhouse where Jack's friends live, but Larry and I spend most of our time in the room they lend us, both of us crying and fighting. He is so remote that I am frightened. I realize that he is not a boyfriend, he is a patient, ill and in need of care. I had no right to ask for even an iota of normalcy.

On Sunday, we drop Larry back in New York and begin the slow ride to Chicago. "You can't help him, Do," Deane says. "It's not good for you."

That fall, I move to Iowa City, Iowa, for the Writers' Workshop. I have put myself in the middle of nowhere, in a beautiful land of churches and pigs, and my days are filled with the long hours of some-one who has nothing to do. The workshop schedules few class hours so students have time to write. But freedom is prison for me. I sit in my apartment and read Bronte, Austen, Hemingway, Colette, smoking cigarettes and trying to turn Larry back into the man I made up. By October he is stable enough to return to the University of Chicago, and on weekends we eat cold pizza in his cell-like room, watching the Watergate hearings. When we say goodbye, he holds me, and asks me to tell him he will be all right.

I do not know that. We spend the year visiting each other, breaking up and then making up again. He is a magnet I can't shake, my idea of passion that I don't want to let go of. One night I tell him we're through. He leaves, drives for two hours, turns around, and comes back. When I hear the knock at my door, I am elated that we can undo what I was so sure of only hours before. He comes in the door, and we can't stop kiss-ing and crying, relieved we don't have to face a future without each other.

But by now I have him confused with the future, and papering this ugly story with the story I want becomes my goal. I won't let this bad story be *my* story.

That spring we decide to get married.

I turn the clock back. I take Larry's mother's ring. I quit the Writers' Workshop.

"You won't become the writer you want to be if you leave," my pro-fessor tells me. Even then I find his pessimism myopic.

Larry and I move into an apartment in Chicago. I opt again for school, the master's education program Larry is completing. I will work with his professors, his classmates. I repeat the mimic I once made of Deane's classes during our third semester at Tufts. I consent to be Larry's intellectual twin, an easier decision than insisting on an identity of my own. Once I have a label—graduate student—I will be safe to take a breath and see who I am: a girl about to marry a man who scares her. Instead of happiness, I feel panic.

Larry is finishing his master's and in the fall will start teaching English at a wealthy public school on the North Shore—a plum assignment, and we are all relieved. But that summer it's clear he's still depressed and withdrawn. To get his attention, I goad him to fight with me.

"Look at this place," I scream. "It's disgusting. Why can't you put your dirty dishes in the sink?" I wave my hands around the filthy hot living room.

"You want me to pick the place up," he says, picking up a big knife.

He's scared me before, his physical violence toward himself. That summer he develops a friendship with another student who is deeply depressed. One night Larry and I go to a baseball game with this man and his date. Larry and I hang back, fighting as we now do so often. A few days later, Larry learns that his friend lay down on a Chicago railroad track in front of train.

"That's me," Larry said, his eyes full of tears. He is morose for days. "Leave me alone," he says when I try to draw him out.

My therapist is becoming more outspoken.

"Larry is a sick guy," she says. "And you are not his therapist. He cannot give you what you need."

Deane comes to visit. She sees what I see: how knocked out Larry is on thorazine, how much weight he's gained, how discordant his laughter is, how much he withdraws.

"I'm scared for you."

I begin to think of another life. I am no longer isolated, and the difference is clear between Tolstoy's dark prince and my classmates who slap optimism on me like mustard. I go to classes, and they are glad to see me. They save seats for me. They listen to my answers. My professor puts As on the top of my papers and tells me I smoke too much. They all remind me of the things I like about myself.

Still, Larry and I are engaged. The whole program knows it, and we get teased constantly about setting a date. Neither of us are willing. Deane and I go to visit my parents, who are silent about my engagement. My father tells me later that he knew we would not last. "He couldn't make you happy," he said. "He didn't know who he was."

After the lights are out, I start to cry. Deane gets up and comes over to sit on the side of the bed.

"Please tell me I won't have to marry him," I say to her.

"You don't," she says. "You shouldn't."

I am so relieved I can feel the breath moving back into my chest.

"So, what am I going to do?"

"Go back to Chicago," she says. "And tell him."

Sick or well, Larry is not the one I want. I ask my therapist how to leave him. She says, "Just tell him you are leaving. Do it quietly and take nothing of his."

I do exactly that. I give Larry back the ring. He doesn't argue. We are so unhappy, it is a relief to think of escaping this damp madness. I tell Larry I am moving out, get in the car and drive to my sister, now living in Ann Arbor, Michigan. It feels simple. But it's not. Larry follows me for one more fight, to keep his life from changing, from emptying more than it has. But this time I mean it and send him home. Deane turns to me, "Your life has just begun," she says. I'm scared, but I try to believe her. We go to her swimming pool, and I float while she holds her hands underneath my back, making sure I don't sink.

Chapter 31

When I return to Chicago, I move out of the place Larry and I share into my friend Cathy's living room. On the day I retrieve my things, I find women's clothing—not mine—in the apartment.

"Whose are these?" I ask Larry, hardly able to speak.

"I met someone, a teacher at work."

"You are disgusting," I say and leave, crying so hard that I can barely drive.

Art, the man Deane is living with in Ann Arbor, who will become her husband, knows John Paul, a new thirty-year-old English professor at Chicago who needs three roommates. So, in a week or so, I move into a small room at the back of a long apartment built in the early 1890s for the Chicago Exposition. John Paul loves to cook Julia Child's recipes and eats one pancake every morning for breakfast, a habit I find charming. He's picked two other roommates, and at night all of us sit together at the dining room table, finishing red wine and coq au vin. I begin to feel something like contentment. So this is friendship. So this is daily life with someone you care about. I take the grocery list, and I buy sugary rolls layered with cinnamon—making one day nicer seems suddenly that simple. A roll on a plate. A recipe from Julia. A glass of wine at a full table.

I begin to see that everyone needs a Dumbo's feather in order to fly, and that everyone eventually will watch it drop. That October I watch my feather swirling to the ground and realize it no longer matters. Slowly both Deane and I have built adult lives apart from each other. At the end of a day of classes, I unlock the door to my dark apartment, and I walk its length to my bright room and realize I am home.

When I see stories about twins who are physically joined at their spines or heads, I think about what it might have been like if Deane and I had been attached. If we had shared a hip, a spine. But all twins are Siamese. All twins are co-joined. Of course, the attachment doesn't show. Anyone can pass a hand between us. But the separation of air from air, of twin from twin, is the operation we face nonetheless.

The lives we saw as indivisible now have markers and limits. Like the stones that make up miles of a wall, our small, day-to-day choices have begun to alter the landscape. Deane is becoming a psychologist, is getting married.

I myself meet a writer with blue eyes and a soft voice. My professor George Hillocks knows I have formed a writers group, and he gives me the phone number of a writer I should meet, Dan Gray. I do nothing about it. And then one April day, still depressed and mooning over Larry, I drag myself from my apartment for a meeting with George. Dan Gray is just finishing his own meeting with George. When he says hello, I feel lighter. His warmth relaxes me, and I notice how handsome he is with dark, curly hair, straight nose, and the light complexion of what are called the *Black Irish*, dark Irish descended from Iberia. I walk home thinking about him instead of Larry.

"What would you think if a woman called you to ask you out?" I asked my roommate John Paul.

He looks at me as if the answer is obvious. "I'd love it," he says. I dither and debate. But I keep thinking about how tranquil just a short encounter with this man had made me feel. So one April afternoon I call Dan Gray and ask him to the movies.

"Only if I can take you to dinner first," he says.

He arrives that afternoon with ice cream bars. I am so nervous, I put mine in the freezer, smoke a cigarette instead. On the way to a Mexican restaurant, he talks about his mother, his sisters. After the movie, Dan invites me to see his T-shirt collection. I actually say yes, and he actually shows me T-shirts with pictures of Blue Boy, of the Pittsburgh Pirates, of tequila sunrises. When he takes me home that night, he kisses me on the stairway, and that's the end of sleep.

I have met my future husband, a man who understands where he begins and ends. Dan's separateness both draws and scares me. He is a listener, but he never adopts my problems. Nor does he hand his to me. He is easy to feel close to, but he has no need to merge. This is new territory for me, and I like it. Because he doesn't lose sight of separateness, the hum of tension from excess intimacy is missing. He's fun, empathetic, sexy, but self-contained.

When we have our first fight, I scream at him like I would my sister. He assumes we're finished.

"That's just the way I fight," I say, shocked that he thinks I am breaking up with him. "I explode, and then it's over."

He's not impressed: his parents fought but always away from the kids. Otherwise, no fighting allowed. Their relationships tread a tranquil surface. My intensity both draws Danny and befuddles him. Too much of me, and he just grows quiet, closes his shutters, and that is that. Not a bit twin-like: when Deane and I fight, we are the cartoons where figures become indistinguishable, one spitball of fury. When I pull Dan there, he gets up, and leaves the room. He requires the dignity one separate person owes another, and that is not part of a twin's repertoire.

Partnership is what I know how to do. I know how to be a piece of another person. For someone who is not a twin, my skill at merger can be baffling, suffocating—as it was for my husband. I marry him in part because he is so clear about boundaries. But I don't always understand how those boundaries work. When he digs a garden the summer after we marry, in seconds I am by his side, watering can in hand. I want to know everything: how to dig, when to plant, what to grow. At night I sit in bed hunched over gardening books. Dan, in the meantime, is not hunching. He is quiet. He puts his hoe in the garage. The more interested I am in tomorrow's carrots, the less time he spends weeding the lettuce. My conclusion is that he is a grouch. How well do I really know this man anyway? Maybe he just gets taciturn. Maybe it has nothing to do with me.

But then my therapist says, "You're used to lockstep. Dan isn't. Isn't it possible you've overwhelmed him, taken what was his? Maybe he likes gardening because it's solitary."

I put my hoe in the garage.

Like Deane, Danny is mostly quiet. In the kitchen, we can choreograph our movements, his setting the table, my tossing the salad. We are—like I am used to and Dan is not—inseparable. At night, we climb in bed, reading our books under a stained-glass window until we fall asleep. On Sundays, Danny carries a tray of coffee and croissants upstairs, and sometimes on cold days we stay there all day in our pajamas reading. When we fight, the fights are about money, about my wish to be elsewhere, in a city with Deane, and my subterranean fury when Dan can't out-Deane Deane.

Two months after Dan and I marry, Deane and Art marry too. Deane is furious that I have scooped her. She and Art decided to marry before Dan and I did. But they are marrying in late May, and I don't want to wait. I am blind to the competition behind my move, the first to marry, the first to get the attention. My drive not to be the one left behind.

I wear a beige dress with a rose pattern, Dan wears a turtleneck and jacket. Deane is my only bridesmaid, Dan's best friend Dominick, his best man. At the end of the service, Dan kisses my cheek, an act of discretion I love.

Deane's wedding is elaborate with a wedding planner that yips at Deane's ankles like a terrier. Deane wears our aunt's white satin wedding gown, and she and Art marry outside in front of the church. All day, the planner pulls them aside for pictures. Deane grieves for months afterward: later she said she knew on her wedding day that she had made a mistake.

Danny and I take the second bedroom in their wedding night suite, like it is a sleepover. No tantrums from Art. No raised eyebrows from Dan. We are twins. And Dan and Art have a strange intimacy too, knowing they each love half of a set, that they both will have to navigate this strange, competing intimacy. In the morning, the pair calls out to us, and we sit on their bed, sharing coffee, before sending them off to the Caribbean.

In June, Dan and I quit our Chicago jobs to move to Ann Arbor, where Deane has moved from Boston to begin graduate school. They too are moving into a new apartment, and together the four of us paint and polish. Once again, Deane and I bridge transition together. We are getting used to living with spouses, but ours is a double adjustment: we are also getting used to sharing each other.

One day Deane drops me off after shopping. I ask her to plan another outing with me, and she snaps:

"I'm married now. Art has to come first, not you."

"You don't have to say that."

"It's true. I do. You make it hard for me."

"Make what hard?"

I am shocked. I don't feel the same need to tell her that Dan is more important than she is. I don't think of him in those terms. He is not my twin. She is. So, I don't have to choose. I have them both.

But in fact, I hate being answerable to Dan. I hate feeling that I have to tell him where I'm going and when I'll be back. I want to disappear and show up when I feel like it. And I'm miserable because we have no money, and I drag the streets looking for work in a town fat with unemployed doctoral students. I land a typing job at a counseling center for mothers and children. From the start, I hate it because all the therapists know my sister: I am the failure, the one who doesn't know what she's doing. Deane is the professional success. I am a typist. I want to wear a sign that says Writer Earning Living. Instead, I hate my bosses.

On Fridays, Deane picks me up at the office, and we zoom off in her rusting Karmann Ghia to a greasy deli where we eat fat pastrami sandwiches and crispy fries, while we discuss how to stop smoking. These are my happiest moments in Ann Arbor—a Friday afternoon with Deane, like our childhood middle-school Fridays when we did the same thing. The feeling is hard to reach back for: stillness, joy, safety. To sit with Deane and know the heart in both of us, so that all we say and don't say makes sense, closes circles, stops time, turns us toward home where we don't have to grow up or away or even for one moment be married.

I think little about Dan's adjustment to all this twinning. He is beyond a good sport: he loves Deane and Art and develops a separate
friendship with each of them. Some days on his way home from work, he
passes their house and stops in for a soda. Dealing with our twinship is
only one on a huge list of adjustments: he misses his own family, his sixteen-year-old sister Judy, his college buddies, his carousing and scout-
ing for women. Now he has this quiet life, with jobs as a night janitor
and a daytime editor. His freedoms are garroted by new everything: jobs,
woman, family, geography. Neither of us yet know quite who we are
apart or as partners. In the kitchen we chop spinach for oysters Rocke-
feller. But later Danny scowls when I turn on the TV: I feel his tensions,
his bouts of anger, but he doesn't articulate them. It's then I know that
he's mourning, as I am. I turn the TV off and smoke in the living room,
drinking coffee, trying to stay out of his way. We can't talk about what
scares us because we're scared of each other, of our psychic overhaul. We
have new names.

Still, Dan is so different from Larry. Mostly Dan is present. He is
not locked up in mental illness. Pain erases humor, and Larry had none.
Dan makes me laugh, he teases me, he does not think of himself as the
world's center. This is Big News. The Foltz men are each the earth's
center. If you screw something up—copying a driver's license, arriving
late, getting a phone number wrong—the sky blackens, and you will pay.
That kind of pique isn't on Dan's radar: his mother never allowed it. In
fact, Dan doesn't even say when he's hungry—I call him a camel—and
he's shocked at how grouchy I get when my tank is empty. In his family,
being hungry is a complaint, a call for personal attention, a way of making yourself the center. Taboo. A man who considers himself last is easy
to be around but not always easy to know. Dan is like that.

Chapter 32

Grief is physical. I hadn't known that. It breaks the blood vessels in my eyelids, and I turn absent-minded. I walk into a room and forget why I'm there. I lose my car keys. I show up at my dentist a day late.

For the first time in my life, I have no interest in food. Appetite is life. I start to eat, and then I am ashamed of the keenness that makes me eat, and my hunger claps shut. I go to a grocery store and I can't think what to buy. I remember to buy milk and orange juice, but good food, luscious food, seems a reproof, a reentry I can't make. I push my cart down aisles that seem enormous, crammed with choices. The last time Deane and I went shopping she eyed a box of glazed cookies. Now I put some in my cart. The store pipes James Taylor, and I put on sunglasses, wondering what people have in their carts besides their normal lives. Hunger—this part of me—has gone elsewhere, lifted into the sky with Deane. I want to memorize someone else's menu: Monday, meatloaf; Tuesday, pot roast. These days Dan and I often eat out: sausage biscuits, soup and sandwiches, fried chicken, food I leave at the side of my plate.

I step outside and the weather's splendor seems tangible, something I could pluck and carry off. For its beauty, I feel both responsible and guilty. I sit outside the library after a morning of sifting through Deane's papers. I spread out in the grass, my sandwich in my lap, and feel the sun on my face. For a few minutes I am on vacation. In Bermuda on a deck chair. I could fall asleep in the sun and wake up lucky.

The day after Deane's funeral I begin a diary, writing in a small notebook

I keep in my purse. Carrying the diary with me on errands, on visits with friends, on my rides to the library, I pretend Deane and I are linked, my voice to hers. One day I tell her about a dream. I am teaching a history class, but I have lost all my notes.

Her history, my notes.

I heard your voice Thursday.

Everyone says I am good at grief. But I am not good.

On the nights we eat at home, I relax at the kitchen table while Dan cooks dinner. I drink a glass of wine and read the letters that have come in the mail. I hate its heap. *I am sorry for your sister's passing.* I hate the letters but embrace them, scouring for anecdotes of Deane—the letter she sent when a friend died, her poker-faced salary negotiations. This is the fabric of loss I hadn't known about. The daily letters, the required answers, the work that keeps me busy, that buries thought. And then the letters slow. And still Deane does not reappear. I wait after each landmark: the end of condolence, the twenty-pound weight loss, the sifted papers. They pass but the horizon each day is the same.

Death robs the future and colors the past. The childhood I once loved with my sister now seems haunted. In pictures, I see her informed by doom, her happiness, her plans a sham. I survived and she didn't. All day I run images of my sister, a machine I can't unplug.

Two months before she died, we sit at a lunch table in Boston. We are eating pasta salad, our packages beside us. Because I loved that moment, her eager face, her curly hair, our happiness, the replay is poison. We ate in innocence with only two months left, a countdown we ignored like Musak. I know I will die with this memory of her instead of thousands of others, and it will circle around me, doom at the center of our plates. After thirty-one years, she is still sitting at that table, frozen in happiness, in what she cannot know. I could have touched her, reached across the table and told her not to go back to Chelmsford. It's easy to think I could.

That night as we listen to the news, I tell my husband that I want to die.

I tell him this as if I am telling him I want to go to the grocery store. I tell him that I will give myself a year, and if I am no better after a year, I will kill myself. I have my feet propped over the edge of our wooden table. The newscaster has just announced the assassination of Anwar al-Sadat, the Egyptian prime minister. I look into my glass of wine and envy Sadat all he knows.

Dan stands a few feet away at the stove. He glances at me, and then he turns back to tossing the vegetables in the wok. He knows, I think, that extremes are what I have to express, but I press him for extremes as well. I don't know what I expect of him when I say I want to die. Do I want him to scream too, to plunge into my sorrow and save me? I think so. What is my motive in telling him? I accept my punishment for being alive. I am ready to face what Deane faced. In the logic of death, duplicating her fate is the only route that makes sense to me.

I know she must be somewhere. I want to step over the line of death and search for her. I want to understand if the flat blue holds her.

I daydream about how to join Deane. Possibility seems to lie in science—or science fiction: I turn back time until I find the first person to make a gun, and I burn his workshop. I carry the fertilized egg of my mother and father and rebirth Deane then stunt my years until our ages are once again a match. I carve through the sky with a machete, hacking my way to the back until I find where she is and pull her down to me before the rip can close. But options don't exist. Instead, I feel the border of panic—like one I felt years earlier, lost from my mother in a department store. I push through racks of Easter coats, dust burning my nose, and still she is not there. I turn toward the sweaters and there's another mother, the wrong mother. I look under skirts at women's legs, but none belong to my parent. I cry and someone takes me to the sales desk and sets me on the counter, and there, across all the hangers and all the other mothers, I see her red curls.

I do not want this lost girl to be my story. I am lost now, but no one props me on a counter. People look at me and hustle past and I put on my dark glasses and go back into the ladies' room, the safest place in

America to cry for free. But clean ladies' rooms also smell like Lowell Hospital. I lean over and read the label on the pink disinfectant.

My stomach waits for resolution. I cut my hair, wear Deane's makeup, write the prologue to her thesis, knit the sweater she'd started. I will be the best mourner ever. And in reward, the phone will ring, and she'll be on the other end to tell me nothing happened.

Chapter 33

In the months after Deane dies, Beth and I become friends. She is a writer I met at a writing conference the year before. We go for a walk, and I tell her about Deane's death. She stops walking and turns to face me on the sidewalk. She does nothing to silence or interrupt me. She doesn't change the subject or squirm or try to comfort me. We sit down to lunch in a restaurant, and she begins talking, her voice almost a whisper. She believes in the spirit, she says, its palpable being. She feels the presence of those she has loved. She talks about a cat that haunts her, whose spirit winds around her trees at night, asking her to notice. She thinks maybe she is a cat herself, come back. She talks about her grandmother's piano. She plays, and her grandmother's soul seeps through the keys. She knows only a gauzy curtain between this world and another one, and the fact that other people don't see this isolates her, saddens her.

I rest my face on my hands and stare at this woman who is speaking my new language. She has red hair and beautiful burgundy clothes, deep purples—Deane's colors, I can't help but notice—and a wide smile outlined in ruby lipstick. She talks about the afterworld as if it were Bloomingdale's, a place to dip in and out of, a place to see your cats. Her heaven is full of unhappiness and sobriety, people and cats scheming a return to the person or animal they loved. They float and inhabit sounds and come in through chimes and out through colors. The place is dense with them, cats hanging in everyone's trees. There is nothing extraordinary about a hovering cat. It's just the way things are, and B puzzles on it and believes it—as do I in my fragmentation. She knows this puts her in another category, slightly Indian maybe. This is why her earthly life is tortured—mean, unhappy marriages, soulless jobs, childhood scoldings. Writing suits her, and ivory notes and food and sky suit her. A sky full of lost cats.

No one else talks to me this way. One person tells me there is no afterlife and so death's the end of Deane. Shelley talks about how Deane would be a vegetable if she had lived. Only Beth has the real conversation, gets down to it, pawing through the gauzy stuff that hangs between my sister and me.

We meet for lunch. We swap manuscripts. We go to literary readings. We shop. And all the time Beth helps me believe in more than the explained. For a year she is my sorcerer, a woman of mystical beliefs whose certainty calms me. I see in her life with her rich husband, her expensive clothes, her nightly wines, an absorbing fantasy. Inside it, I step out of myself and become another person, someone I make up. I want to grow as close to Beth as I had been to Deane.

Dan goes along gamely, perhaps relieved that I have a focus, a new friend. I only realize later how appalled his Pittsburgh Blue Collar must have been as we rode with Beth and Russ in their Jaguar to New Orleans, sipping white wine out of flutes in the back seat. We head into Big Easy restaurants that have white tablecloths and trout *meunière*, and I am happy to pretend this is what life is. Dan and I run early in heat that mugs us, slaps our chins and thighs, and leaves us enervated and sick, facing more red beans and rice, the rich seasoning of the world Beth and Russ let us peek into. Russ is a businessman, very grown up. He's a Southern gent, and Dan gets along with him fine. But these are not Dan's people—no Italian loaves here, or beers to pour down, and bars to belly up to. He knows I'm somewhere else with grief, and he follows along like my own Secret Service, letting me wander, so long as I don't get hurt.

But as the months slip by, the haze begins to clear. I move from shock to something else, to the beginnings of who I am without Deane. I realize that Beth is as lost as I am. She has married a man she doesn't know or love but who has money, and she uses the money to keep a distance between her and whatever she doesn't want to feel. And my intensity, my longing that she become Deane, is not appealing to her.

"I don't want to be your family. Your sister," she says to me one day while I weep at the table.

"Why are you so mad at me?" I ask her, beginning to shake.

"I'm not mad. You're the one who's mad. You're mad at your father, you're mad at my husband, you're mad at Danny. And I won't help you. I can't help you."

For the first time I realize how scared she is, that I might look at her and see nothing there. Or see her fear. Or see a sister she wants no part of. I'm not even sure. But I do see a coldness, like her heart has twisted backward in her chest. She's sorry she told me about the cats, about her grandmother, about the writing life she dreams of. She orders another glass of wine.

I tell her I plan to take a job managing a modern dance company.

"You are wasting your life," she comments.

"Well, I'm not," I say. "I need a job."

"This isn't about money. You are a writer."

"But it is."

She frowns. I am an affront; my choices are an affront. I am confused by her attitude. I am a writer whether I take a job or not, except with a job I can pay bills. I push my salad away and drink my wine.

I tell her Danny and I want a baby. I push on, as if I can bludgeon her into intimacy.

"I don't know if we can still be friends if you have a baby," she says. She hates parents who take their kids to restaurants, who speak English to French waiters.

"Did you just say you can't be friends if I have a baby?"

"I am not your sister. I am not your family. We are not related," she says again.

I get up from the table and go into the ladies' room. I go inside a stall and sit down to cry, my usual spot. When I go back out, I will leave because our friendship is over. I will leave because sorcery and denial and friends with red hair and burgundy clothes cannot bring Deane back.

A year has passed since Deane died, and now I know she's dead, we're dead. I am no longer looking for pink skies or wondering if her soul is lodged in a dead squirrel, or perched with a cat on the branch over my head. I no longer study whether the air is just the gauze that separates us. Mostly, I just don't think: instead I move into another life, and I've picked up my bag of sanity where I parked it a year ago, I want to believe Deane is with me: I always will. But I'm no longer trying to figure out where time's portal is or who invented gunpowder.

My husband and I stop seeing Beth and her husband. I begin to run road races and gain weight. I take a job managing a modern dance company, keeping books, scheduling performances, writing paychecks. It's tough to brood about loss and balance a business at the same time. The company has dozens of performances at the 1982 World's Fair in Knoxville, and each day I walk to the outdoor stage where five dancers spin to Appalachian music, and the world opens. In one piece, dancers slide over a huge rubber ball painted like a watermelon. I want to join them, their young catapults. The people I meet don't know I had a twin sister who died.

I pull myself toward August 14, the one-year anniversary of the shooting, as if the calendar were a rope I climb hand over hand. It is a kind of finish line, the end of a long race, and I know some magic lies over the line if I can reach it. I've been told the first year is the toughest. So I believe that on August 15, I will wake up whole. Because I have grieved so well, because I've never taken to my bed or worn my bathrobe around the house past noon, I will get Deane back. I'll wake up and see Deane sitting next to me in her pajamas.

I do not want to be in the house on August 14. So Danny and I go camping. The campground is shabby, as crowded with ill-kempt children as a grocery store parking lot. In the spot next to us, the grounds man keeps roosters that wake me at dawn. I walk outside and watch the light cast across the river. I crawl back in next to Danny and stick my cold feet under his legs. In a few minutes I'm cozy again, but I don't fall back to sleep. I open the rear flap of the tent and stare out. I know I cannot escape this day by sleeping outside under a tent. The fact of my sister's death has turned into a mountain. I can run into it, walk around it, respect it. But I cannot bury it. It is my landscape.

When Dan wakes up, we walk to the showers and on the way pass two girls playing nearby, waiting while their mother showers. Their identical faces turn up as we pass, and I ask them if they are twins. I am a twin, too, I say, and they giggle into their hands. I see them there, and they are the black crows, the song on the radio, the pink sky of Deane's messages.

Chapter 34

Over the years, I saw many news clips about workplace killings but none about therapists whose patients shot them—until I finally had to find them, to know how others went through what Deane had, what my family had. It wasn't hard to scratch up the unsurprising news that Deane and her colleagues were not the first or last to suffer a patient's wrath. The shooting at Stoney Brook was the third violent episode against physicians in Lowell in six years. One New Year's Eve, a doctor, his wife, and son were murdered in their home. At St. Joseph's Hospital, where Deane was treated, a young doctor was shot and paralyzed by a dialysis patient angry over a change in the hours of his treatment. In the fallout after Stoney Brook, doctors talk about carrying guns. A nearby mental health center places guards at every door. Another checks to make sure Palmer was never treated there, would never show up to shoot their doctors in the head.

Deane knew something about patient violence. In 1970, her first year out of college, she worked as a live-in youth worker in a group home for troubled teenagers. The job worried her: she was untrained to help the girls whose pain was so apparent. She drove them to activities, and they asked her to blare the radio, swaying and snapping to its emotional blasts, and she saw how crucial music was to them, a lone note of inclusion. They recognized her empathy, moved closer like wobbly fawns, and yet one night they dragged Deane by her hair out into the snow, ran back to the house, locked her out, and set the place on fire.

Deane came to my apartment the next evening, sitting in my wooden rocker while she told me the story.

"I have to quit," she said, slumped in the chair, her blue-jeaned legs in front of her, her face marked by sadness and disappointment. "I don't want to be a quitter."

I said something helpful like, "Are you nuts? You have to quit. They're setting the house on fire, pulling you around by your hair. Quit, quit, quit," I chanted. She laughed, but she still felt like a failure.

She quit not long after that. But the hair-pull clinched her application to graduate school. And as she waded into graduate school, treating her first patients, she had some who scared her. With one, her bowels cramped during each session, so much that she often had to leave and run to the bathroom during the hour. Call it countertransference, a physical reaction aligned with the patient. Is this how her patient felt too?

Still, she never expected to be killed by a patient. That was Hollywood stuff, not the reality of treating middle-class neuroses.

A Mick Stevens's *New Yorker* cartoon: the patient is lying on a couch, and the psychiatrist sits across from him in a chair, his foot in a cast on a stool, his head in bandages. The caption: "You left your demons here last week."

It's funny but also real—and one possible explanation why Palmer did what he did, his shootings the deposit of demons he couldn't bear.

Such violence against therapists is not uncommon. In 2003, researchers at Georgia State University gathered surveys from a thousand mental health professionals in Georgia that revealed fourteen thousand physical or psychological assaults by patients. A third of the professionals had feared for their lives at least once. That jibes with other studies suggesting that 60 percent of professionals will be assaulted during their careers, a figure that hasn't changed since Deane's death.

In one account of an attack, a patient shoots an arrow at her therapist while the therapist dives behind a chair. "You aren't going to tell my mother about this, are you?" the patient asks, just before trying again to shoot him with an arrow. In another, a psychiatrist is treating a former policewoman with a history of violence who is hearing voices. The doctor begins tucking a gun in his belt during their appointments. One day the patient lays her purse across her lap, her hand in the purse. The doctor moves his hand closer to his gun. In the end he is able to talk her out of a showdown. But she does have a loaded gun in her purse.

The reasons for such aggression are many. Some therapists feel they get too close to a patient too fast, which may feel threatening. Certainly it appears that Palmer revealed more than he could live with or let his doctors live with. Other therapists speculate that patients transfer the anger they feel toward someone else—a parent, a spouse—to the therapist. As Palmer may have done shortly after fights with his wife, his mother, his friend.

Violence and disconnection swing along together like lovers. A person who traffics in violence is also one whose relationships sour.

For doctors who survive patient assaults, tranquility is elusive. Many survive only to combat post-traumatic stress disorder—and those with the worst physical injuries are the most battered emotionally.

After Deane's death, I thought of Deane's friend and colleague, Barbara Kaplan, who lost her eye in the Chelmsford shooting as the lucky one, the one whose family got to see her recover in the hospital. I had never met her, and I didn't want to meet her. I didn't send her a note or flowers or any acknowledgment of how much she and her family suffered. She had scooted under the rope, she had made it out, and I couldn't forgive her.

A year or two later, I saw a piece Barbara wrote for the *Boston Globe* about the incident, about violence turned on mental health professionals. Again, I felt angry. Her voice seemed controlled, professional, reflective. Too reflective, too controlled. It made me angry to read about that day from her point of view, as if she owned a part of what happened to Deane that I did not, as if she didn't see it adequately or accurately. But no one knew that day more completely than she—and perhaps it was that I couldn't stand, that she was there and I was not. That she survived and we as "we" did not.

When I met her four years after the shooting at the dedication of a Tufts University site named for Deane, I could barely speak to her. My reaction was unreasoning, primal, one that didn't honor my sister's friendship with Barbara. But I didn't think about that. It took me years to realize how angry I was, not just at Barbara, but in my bones: they were made of anger.

Only years later did I learn how much Barbara suffered: she had five eye operations over eight years; the first one took eight hours. Her sinuses were fractured, she had constant sinus infections, a healthy person now always sick. The doctors had to graft a new bone socket to hold her prosthetic eye in place. Her new fake eye sat too low, the wrong shape, its ugliness her daily reminder of guilt and fear. The world felt dangerous, like anything could happen at any time. "I just felt so scared. I couldn't count on safety in the world."

She felt guilty about surviving. For a long time she wouldn't amend the scar that surrounded her damaged eye; she felt she deserved to wear it.

"My survival guilt was the hardest part because it felt so beyond rationality. And that made it hard for me to think clearly. I got it in my mind that your family wished me dead," she told me.

A newlywed, she was no longer the independent bride her husband knew: instead he found himself consoling a person who was needy and clinging.

"I wasn't much fun. But Joel had a good way of dealing with it. He would say, 'This isn't Barbara. It's a product of the shooting.' He didn't take it in. He didn't see this as the real me."

She went into therapy, but the therapist who knew the pre-shooting Barbara couldn't understand how profoundly she had changed.

"I thought, 'Is he trying to hurt me?'"

She began to talk with the woman who had been her consultant. And when Barbara began to talk about having a baby, the consultant discouraged her. "Oh, maybe you should wait a year," she said. When Barbara told her she didn't deserve to have her eye fixed, the woman answered, "If this were your daughter, what would your advice be?"

Barbara had the operations.

Two years after the murders, she began to see patients again—mostly women—in her home. She became active in a victims movement, seeing crime victims. Then an angry man showed up and she quit, retreating to telephone assessments for a national organization, referring phone patients to therapists.

"I don't have to deal with crises," she says.

After three years, she had a daughter, Miriam, whose name means waters of strength.

"Before her birth, it felt like I was on a death track. That was all I thought about: death. But Miriam put me on a life track, and my life is all about life. Her birth marked a division in my life."

Talking to Barbara so many years after the shooting, I could see what Deane must have seen in her. The conversation was painful for her, and yet she offered it to me. She fetched up details of the shooting and talked about her friendship with Deane.

"The first thing we would do when we got a moment at Stoney Brook," she says, "was review our schedules to see if we had time for a cup of coffee. She was a lot of fun. Early on, she noted how messy my bedroom was, and she said her goal was to have a bedroom as messy as mine."

That was Barbara: for a moment she gave me Deane.

Chapter 35

When Deane dies, I turn to Dan again. He is comforting, but he is complete on his own. He has no wish to become part of a whole, to confuse himself with me. His clarity rankles me. I want him to behave as Deane might, to explain how I can live without her, to help me imagine a future. The world is vacant, and the span of years endless. I want Dan to erase that picture.

A month after Deane's death, I sit on the sofa and begin to cry. Dan sits across from me in his rocking chair. He watches me, but he does not move. He wants our life back.

Before Deane's death, no one could have accepted my twin-ship with more grace and generosity than he had. He knew he would share me. He never insisted I choose; he is grown up in that way, a mensch. How he managed it, I'm not certain: the Saturday morning phone calls, the visits, the flap of excitement when Deane and I were together.

Dan stepped in to play another part. But as my life emptied of Deane, the landscape of my relationship with Danny shifted. He was there to accept the shift—from the moment I slumped against his shoulder at Lowell Hospital. *His the foot on earth.*

In those first months, Dan's insistence on the present makes me angry. It is also his gift, his reminder of the day's steady pulse. One day when I try to crawl back into bed, he proposes a hiking trip. We dress in flannels and blue jeans and go to the banks of a nearby stream. We sit together on the bank and look at the sun highlighting the water. "There she is," Danny says to me.

Each morning he drops me off at the Oak Ridge Library, where I haul a box of Deane's papers, spending each morning going through them, deciding which to copy for family and friends, which to toss. In the car, we say little, but Danny is comfortable with quiet the way other people are with prattle. And he has patience. If I'm not my querulous self, well, he won't pick a fight.

At noon he picks me up for lunch at a nearby restaurant. He looks at my the red swollen skin around my eyes but talks about which soup to have, what little bratty thing one of his students did, which Emily Dickinson poem no one understands. Sometimes he maddens me, but I also love his anchor, his thoughtful knowledge that the daily will keep me from floating away.

Of course, he is grieving too. Deane was his close friend. One year for Christmas, she sent him sunflower seeds from the sunflowers he'd planted in Ann Arbor that he never got to see in bloom because we had moved that year to Knoxville. Another year, she sent him a soap carving of the Incredible Hulk, which made him laugh out loud. He found her accomplished and paradoxical in her quiet modesty, identified with her silence, knows that they both puzzled over my spitting tongue. But he says nothing to me about his sadness. My guess is that I left him no room for it.

"I'd like to go for a run," he says. "Along the river."

"I dunno. I don't have any energy," says the grump.

"You'll feel better, fatty," he says. "I'll wait."

I strap on my shoes, and I see he's got two fishing poles in his hands. We jog down to the river. He lopes, holding the poles as easily as a spear, as if it's nothing to jog with two rods. We sit on the bank, where I am unimpressed by the prospect of fishing. But it is a beautiful day, the sun warm on my skin, the air fragrant with river moss. He tosses my line in and hands me the pole.

"Now, just tell me when you feel a tug," he says.

I don't change my expression. But I take the pole.

Then a weight, a solid pull in water.

"It's tugging," I scream.

"Okay, start reeling in, real slow," he says, smiling.

I see a flash of silver coming up through the water—mercury on the tip of a thermometer.

"It's a fish. A fish," I scream, reeling.

I pull it in, a tiny sliver of silver flapping on the bank. Danny scoops it. "A sunfish," he says, grinning at me. He knows he hooked a piece of the day for me, made me sit still and feel it, fall into, get hooked by it, as cleanly as the fish did. That's what he does: he doesn't need to talk, and sometimes that's confusing. But what he does is not.

I stand outside what I understand intimacy to be, staring at it. Do other people—people who are not twins—feel what I feel? What are the rules? How close can I get? How far should I step back? I resume days of silence like those when Deane and I first separated. I learn how alone other people are. So alone they don't even know it.

I do not give up being a twin. For the next year, the next five years, I look at my life as a shredded puzzle. Without Deane, what makes sense?

I play both parts, mine and Deane's. What would Deane say now? What would she think? Practiced, I spin out her answers. The deception is comforting. It keeps me with her. It keeps me from abandoning her. What haunts me is that I wasn't with her the morning she was shot. I replay the moment, knocking her out of the way, or stepping in front of Palmer. It is not possible that Deane faced death without me. I want to save her, and I want to die. Both things out of reach and unalterable.

Yet life is oddly vivid. The sun never brighter, the autumn colors sharper. I shop for shoes, feeling almost happy and then reprehensible. How could I live? Even now, thirty years later, when something extraordinary happens to me, guilt can strike first.

For a long time after Deane died, my parents call me *Deane*. Other people do too, people who knew Deane better than they know me. That fall when I visit Deane's best friend, Sarah, we go to a ball park, and a woman who knew Deane waves up to me in the stands:

"Hi, Deane," she yells. Then I see her face crumple as she remembers. She hunches her shoulders and turns away.

No one does this this to be cruel. They do it because they'd always done it—called that face Deane. I do it too. When I look in the mirror, I see not my own face but Deane's. When I start to cry, Deane cries too. I lie on the bed and try to think who died. To answer, I have to understand who I am: all Deane, part Deane, part Dorothy, all Dorothy. What is confusing is that I have died and remained.

Deane was a good listener, a quiet observer. What seemed unmanageable acquired some of her composure and became less overwhelming. Now, after her death, I struggle to do this for myself. I learn to enjoy stillness, to be alone with my thoughts. At thirty-two, I begin life as a singleton, a life most people take for granted, but one as mysterious to me as my twin-ship is to others. I wade into unmapped space.

I do this in part by immersing myself in work. I have trouble writing, but I'm invited to be on a statewide arts panel and become involved in various conferences. The arts are all mine—not the arena Deane had carved out for herself. I love the people I meet: jesters walking on stilts, whittlers fashioning knife handles, an actor costumed like Einstein. Just enough outside Earth's boundaries for me to feel happy. Grown-ups who earn their livings dancing. Acting, writing. Here is an identity. Danny too is a writer, so stepping into that spot feels both separate from Deane but aligned with Danny. WE could do this—the "WE" my safe place as I test single waters.

None of the people I meet at these meetings and conferences know I was a twin and have lost her. I have to explain nothing, and I welcome the blank slate. I meet two artists, women involved in a modern dance company that needs a full-time manager. I admire their gravity, their insistence on art. I apply for the job—and get it. On some days, my job is to watch their performances at the 1982 World's Fair in Knoxville. I sit in the bleachers watching the dancers, their artistry, their joy in the dances. At night I write poetry and try to let their joy in. I try to wear a single path in my brain where I feel steady on my own.

Chapter 36

When my mother leaves the alcohol treatment center, her tremors do not stop. Her hands curl up, unworking. And she still walks like she's been drinking. For months my father takes her to doctors who test her brain, her lungs, her heart. After a year, she is diagnosed with amyotrophic lateral sclerosis—ALS or Lou Gehrig's disease—a progressive wasting disease that attacks muscle neurons until its victim is no longer able to breathe. Bit by bit she loses control of her body. Now my father's work is finding specialists and nursing homes.

Within months, when she can no longer breathe on her own, she has a silencing tracheotomy and moves into a nursing home. I visit Philadelphia, and my father and I make the half-hour drive to the nursing home, a drive he makes twice a day. I walk into the home and hear the groans and cries of patients in pain or with dementia, sounds that mingle with cheerful greetings of nurses behind the desk and attendants rolling carts of food. Inside my mother's room, I see her illness: her hair white at the roots, her cheeks sunken to her jawbone, her neck wrapped with gauze where the breathing tube emerges. As I lean over her, both of us begin to cry. Outside her window, a cherry tree is beginning to bud.

Five to 10 percent of ALS is inherited, and doctors don't yet understand who is susceptible. But as I look at my mother's wasted face, I see the years of grief and drinking fall like a caul on her immune system. Every day she asks when she will go home.

On bad days—and most of them are—my father fixes himself a

scotch and soda and drinks it in the car as he drives. On the way, he stops to buy my mother a hot chocolate chip cookie, a treat she loves but sometimes chokes on. The nursing home says no more Cokes, and that is when I cry, thinking of my coffee-swilling, Coke-loving mother without one. Until my father insists that they give her Coke again. What is the point? Every day at five before my father arrives, my mother asks a nurse to put her lipstick on. One day, on the long drive there, I ask my father what drew him to my mother so long ago.

"She was a mystery. I never knew exactly who she was or what she felt about me. I'd leave her, and we'd be so in love . . . and then I'd get a Dear John letter. She was so elusive."

He picks up his scotch from the car cup and drinks.

"And she was so beautiful. One night I was in the lobby of a hotel waiting for her. And when she walked down the stairs, every man in the lobby turned to look at her."

He is certain he is going bankrupt. The insurance coverage only goes so far, and there is none for catastrophic illness. He hires a billing firm to sort through the medical paperwork.

"I wake up at night. It's that unreasoning fear. Your mother wants to come home. But I can't afford it. She would have to have a pulmonary specialist there to clear her lungs. I can't do it. "

Every day she fixes him with a look and writes on her board, "When can I leave?"

He changes the subject.

Her friends make a videotape: each one steps before the camera, unsure what to say. Only Warren, the minister, is himself, at ease with dying, his cheer and warmth palpable next to the discomfited others.

I can't blame them. I can hardly talk to her myself. The daily chitchat that usually fills conversation seems trivial. But not to my mother. She still wants to show me the cards she gets, to find out about Danny, to know where I get my clothes. When Dad and I arrive late one afternoon, she makes it clear by the set of her jaw and the bore of her eyes that she is furious—and that, despite her inability to speak, she is not speaking to us. Even as she dies, she makes me remember the mother I dislike, the one outside reach.

The attendants come in, and they see an old woman, not my mother. What I see is still the face from my childhood.

The night before she dies—seven years after my sister's death—she takes her hands, curls the fingers in a fist, and lifts them, thumbs up for my father.

My brother gives the eulogy. Again, I pick the dress, the shoes, the beads. He tells this story: One day when he visits Mom, he is wearing two Band-Aids on his face to cover small skin cancers he has had removed. With effort, she lifts her arm as if by pulley and places her suspended finger on her own face in the two identical spots. She is dying. But she wants to know what's wrong with his face.

My brother and I run together and talk more often. We talk about whether we believe in life after death, and we talk about family. We run up the stairs of the Philadelphia Art Museum, turn around, and pretend we are each Rocky, jogging in place, holding our fists in the air.

My brother widens his life. For years he has worked in downtown Philadelphia, an arrangement he despises. Now he focuses on his dream of moving his business to rural Maine. He buys a house on the water in Rangeley. In the mornings, he makes calls. In the afternoons, he steps onto the cross-country ski trails he has helped build. Or he heads down to the water for an hour's row. We know what Deane, her early death, has given us.

Chapter 37

By the end of the first year, my grief and fear and loneliness find their way to a wish for children. Before Deane died, Dan and I were ambivalent about becoming parents. Dan had helped raise a sister ten years younger than himself. He already knew the demons it could produce in him: the responsible attachment he felt for his sister, the tedium of caring for her, the fury she stirred when he could not make her behave. He was her perennial babysitter, the baby he turned away from only to watch her fall down stairs, cutting her chin open. He still carried the guilt he felt and anger for that guilt. He knew much more than I did about the surrender children demand, their possession.

I had fears too—that children would doom me to a wordless life of domestic toil. It was an issue we had put away before Deane's death. But in the months after Deane died, as I work out schemes for getting Deane back, I remember genetics.

It's not the wisest way to decide on children and not an ideal entry for any baby, born to assuage his mother's grief. But I am not thinking about that. I believe that a baby will heal me, will grow my life back, a new limb on my tree. Our baby will have my genes, Deane's genes—as close to Deane as I can get.

My husband's ideas shift too. He and I both feel more vulnerable, older, although we are only in our early thirties. Our first son is Dan's gift to me, of life after so much death.

I love being pregnant, the roll of it, the tight drum of growth. I picture a little girl inside me, Deane inside me. I see myself in a white gown rocking my red-haired baby on the porch. The crickets sing. The dark settles at my feet.

But I do not have a baby girl. I have Jacob, with round, red lips that remind me of a rose. Because he is born with the cord wrapped twice around his neck, he must spend his first twelve hours in an incubator. I am not allowed to hold him. Instead I scrub my arm up to the shoulder and stick it through the portal in the glass plate to pet his head.

The next day, when the nurse tells us it's time to go home *with the baby*, I sputter: "But . . . but . . . you have to show me how to change a diaper." We received more instruction when we took home a kitten.

At home, I stand next to Jacob's crib. He is dressed in yellow-footed pajamas. He lies on his stomach, his head turned to the wall as he sleeps. I gaze down at him, looking for signals from another world. I see that he has touched a far side of the sky, and now his memory floats away from him like seeds from a pod. Behind his closed, fluttering lids he watches what he forgets, what I have forgotten. I want to pull from him all that he knows. But what I see is his body planted here for me. I look for Deane, and I cannot find her. She is not anywhere here. I know I cannot predict the ways my life will grow back or the loves that will be in it.

The day we bring Jacob home from the hospital, Dan goes into his study to write, afraid Jacob will steal this from him. Jacob affects him as he feared: he feels the world now owns him. He must conform, earn a better living, put on a school face to be the respectable father Jacob deserves. This makes him grouchy. We are like a Laurel and Hardy routine, so ignorant of babies. Dan reads aloud from Dr. Spock about how to change a diaper—we retain nothing from the nurse—as I bend over Jacob, hoping he won't pee in my face. Dan is awed by Jacob's beauty, his responsiveness, his tiny hand folding and unfolding. But he is also miserable in attachment, another corner of his life nailed down. Still, as with everything else, he is in some ways an easy parenting partner, quick to get up in the night to bring Jacob to me for nursing, quick to babysit when I go stir crazy.

Both of us hate the confinement and fatigue that comes with a baby. One morning we walk toward the car and realize we have left Jacob behind in the house. Our bridge to our new parenting life is not easy to build. We solve this by taking Jacob with us everywhere—to the Smokies, to restaurants, to Boston to see Deane's best friend, Sarah. I learn a new side of Dan that I have not seen: his impatience with childish behavior, even from a child. At night we fight over sleep like starving people fight over food.

In the early mornings, I go running while Danny watches Jacob. I run along a country road, past the tall grasses, past the Williams's cows that turn their heads to stare as I pass. As I run, the sweet smell of Jacob sweeps around me—on my hands, on my clothes. I am happy to be outside, to be in the fresh air where I am free, where I pretend my life is not divided into blocks of a baby's slumber. Once again, who I am confounds me. The person I'd found after Deane died has slipped away, and in her place is this caged mother. I am not the mother in the white rocker. And Jacob is not the baby I was prepared to nurture. Jacob's first movements are to roll away from me. He wants down, and he wants to play, not cuddle. I see my life stretching into his adulthood, numbly rocking him to sleep while my tears drip down his back. What made me think a baby would heal me? What made me think that I, still tangled in my sister's skin, could untangle someone else?

I hate being a mother, not knowing who I am. I hate my torn, swollen body. Except I love the way Jacob smells, like cinnamon. I love his round, smooth face, and his open lips. What I despise is me, still trapped on earth, still unchained from heaven, still floating through this slow life.

To mother well, you must know who you are. But no woman knows who she will be as a mother. Those first few months, I am so busy looking for Deane that I almost miss Jacob. I am too unhappy, too numbly pessimistic to understand the way my life has opened.

Then I take Jacob to the doctor's for a six-week checkup. When the nurse pricks his toe for a blood test, he clings to my chest, turns his face up to mine, and my soothing stills his sobs. He has made me his mother, in spite of my grief.

By the time I become pregnant with my second child seventeen months later, I have become a different person—weary, less hopeful, but no longer chronically grieving. I have set my hopes on a child whose gifts are beauty and intelligence but not warmth. I have asked too much. Neither Dan nor I want a second child. So this time we deliberate as if we are buying a dryer, our expectations practical.

"A second child will divert Jacob, take his mind off of us," I argue.

"Another baby will be twice as hard," says Danny, his spirits sinking, as he sees I am shifting another way.

"I don't want Jacob to be an only child."

We succumb glumly, as if we are choosing the less offensive of two unsavory choices. But secretly, I am glad: I think of this new child as a playmate for Jacob, another branch to the tree I am growing. Although I now know that I am not a mother who likes babies, I also know I will just get through this first part. I will do my own healing and my own mothering. I will become a mother I can recognize and accept.

I birth Matthew Deane, a snuggly baby who likes nothing better than to sit on my lap. I gaze at his wide face, his big eyes, feeling his stillness move into me. It is Christmas, and when we get home, we rock in front of a warm fire. Jacob leans into my lap, cooing.

"Want to go see *101 Dalmatians* tomorrow, just you and me?" I ask him.

He squeezes up his shoulders and fists and nods into my face, into his brother's face.

"But not Matthew," he says.

"Not Matthew."

I had thought I could grow my life back by duplication. What else would a twin think? But I was looking behind me. What I didn't trust was the unimaginable future, that life would grow back in two tow-headed boys, in the moist smell of cinnamon.

Deane and I had always pictured being mothers together. We fantasized that our children would look just alike, as we had. We would be the refuge for each other's children, the good aunt they could talk to when Mom acted the witch. I would be the feisty aunt who encouraged the kids to mouth off, who secretly applauded their rebellions. And Deane would be the soothing, wise aunt. The listener when I was squawking.

We would spend summers together at a beach, the children knotting and unknotting on the sand like the kites they let soar. Deane's children would know me almost as well as they know Deane, as my children too would know her.

Deane had always wanted children more than I had. When she first held her best friend Sarah's baby, her face carried the wonder and surprise and longing she felt. She was always much better at putting herself aside than I was, able to lean toward the needs of others without losing herself. What better trait for a mother?

Now I had children whom I hoped would carry me back to her, whom I hoped she'd met in some nether world, whose watery pre-birth lives held a touch of Deane's secrets.

But after Jacob's birth, I lost myself. I was nothing like the mother I imagined that Deane or I would be. I hadn't given birth to Deane but to the hardest parts of myself, a baby who couldn't wait to get off my lap, who couldn't sleep. I'd rock him for an hour, his eyes shut, but the moment the rocker stopped, his eyelids shot up like over-wound window shades, and we would have to start over.

Then I had Matthew, aglow with Deane's uncertain sweetness. Her tiny vein repeats between his eyebrows. He carries her round face. I realize when I look at Jacob and Matthew that I have birthed Dorothy and Deane.

That's not uppermost in my thoughts as I raise them. They are originals too. But when Jacob charges through the yard, his play sword aloft, crying, "Thundar, the Barbarian," my fingers itch to call Deane, to paint the portrait of her bossy sister—Moi— imprinted on my little boy and hear her laughing. And when at night I say to Matthew, "I'm so glad I have you," and his whole body wriggles under the sheets from his happiness, I feel how absent—and present—my sister is. I cannot tell her of this one moment, her love so clearly in his.

For my sons, their missing aunt is an abstraction. Little Americans, they tune in quickly to material losses. Aunt Deane is the absence of a pile of presents they will never get. I admit I feed this: it's somehow comforting to tell them how she would have spoiled them with dinosaurs and Legos and homemade cookies. As I'd tell them this, they'd stare, their little mouths slightly open, unable to imagine an aunt who looked just like Mama—and who also teetered around with a sack of toys as big as Santa Claus's.

As they got older and made friendships, Deane became the dramatic story to tell their friends: their mom had an identical twin—and more than that, she was murdered. When you're seven, that's a big story. When you're sixty-three, that's a big story.

They asked repeatedly, as if I never answered quite well enough, "What was she like, Mama? Would we have known who you were?"

When I show them pictures of the two of us together, and they pick out the wrong one as their mother, they are shocked and unsettled, shaking their heads, even as they snuggle more closely to me.

My guess is that they don't want to think too much about my sister, for if she died, then surely I could too. What they do understand is that there is a hole in my life. And if there is a hole in mine, then one opens in theirs as well.

When they are in their early teens, the news show *20/20* features a Valentine's Day story of twins. The producer had found the published story I had written about losing Deane and called to interview me, then invited me to be on the show. The night the tape aired, Dan was out of town. Jacob made popcorn, and the boys led me to the sofa, sitting on either side of me like tensile bodyguards, sensing they must protect me. My loss was too much to expose—they understood that as only an adolescent could—and they were scared for me, and perhaps for themselves.

The popcorn grew cold in the bowl. The clip began by showing moving pictures our mother had taken of Deane and me in our teens, the first time Jacob and Matthew had ever seen them. There we were for them at last, the mama and the aunt, arm in arm, walking and laughing, our curly red hair bouncing on our shoulder blades. So, we existed after all.

I had flown from Knoxville to Boston for that interview, which took place in the dormitory Deane and I shared our freshman year at Tufts University. The reporter and I sat facing each other in the large common room where Deane and I had lounged, gone to Christmas parties, waited for our parents' visits. I walked down the hallway to Deane's old room and thought how much shabbier, how much smaller it seemed.

Between takes, the reporter and producer talked, the producer urging the reporter to ask me about the picture of Deane and me I was holding, our two identical profiles, our hands clasped. He asks me about separation, and I laugh, pointing to the picture, saying "As you can see, we weren't making much progress."

After this part of the interview, the reporter and I drive to the place in Harvard Square where Deane and I once spoke of dying.

"If something happens to me, you have to promise me that you will be all right," said Deane.

"I will," I promised her. "I will."

The producer and I then drive to Chelmsford, to the shopping center where Stoney Brook, Deane's counseling center, had been. The reporter arrives in a separate car, eager to leave once this segment finishes. We walk inside, the cameraman at the end of the hall, as Deane had been, as Palmer had been. He films the reporter and me as we walk toward him. The offices are unassuming, small and dark. They have a prefab feel, as if the building had been thrown up fast to house an insurance agency or a car rental place. So unassuming it is hard to picture violence here. So small that it's easy to see how Palmer made a rush down the hall, easy to see how intimate the violence was: no grand foyer where bullets could ricochet, a space for easy marks.

Tonight, my sons know what they've lost, what I have lost, but they also think our life, my life is inoculated with happiness. When they are with me, and we're visiting, say, Vancouver, and we're standing in the Granville Market, surrounded by coffee and flowers and smoked salmon and cinnamon doughnuts that we eat with a view of the Strait of Georgia, Matthew says, "Mama's got her blind happiness." He means my giddy state when anything might happen, when I might strike up with a stranger, or do a little jig, or just bump into anyone or thing because I'm so absorbed by glee.

At those moments, I feel known as only Deane knew me—Dorothy and her blind happiness. If they see it and share it, somehow I feel she does too. They are her genes as much as mine, not my twin, but they know me almost as she did. I am surely no longer alone. At those moments, too, they know—consciously or not—that their mama survived her worst loss, and so they will too.

Chapter 38

My thirties are the decade I will never remember, a blur of deaths and births, and suddenly I am forty. In the decade after Deane died, I tried on friends the way other women try on shoes—and none of them fit. I had the perfect friendship template no one could match. Mine was a harsh indictment: you were either Deane or you weren't (and of course no one ever was). I never voiced comparisons, and for a long time I was unaware that I'd made them. I only knew that as I tried on friendships, I felt unsafe, I hid, and invariably I wound up angry.

At forty, though, I found a friend, Ellen, who looked like me: reddish curly hair, a bunch of energy on a long, thin frame. We looked at the world the same way, and she asked me to lunch over and over, even as I turned her down to go swimming instead. But she persisted, teasing me about my reluctance. Danny and I both liked her husband as well, and soon the four of us were eating dinner, swimming, and picnicking together. Sometimes Ellen and I sat on a sofa, slumped down in the seats, giggling, knocking into each other as we laughed. When we did, I felt a memory stir: *I remember this, this is how I felt with Deane.*

The friendship scared me too: this woman meant too much to me too fast. And even as I realized that she and another woman, Lynn, were my first real friends since Deane, I tempered my happiness with worry. Ellen and Lynn and I were a trio: a trio was what I was good at. My idea of friendship encompassed trios: all during my childhood, Deane and me and a friend. I knew how to do this.

After a year or two, Ellen got a new job in San Francisco and Lynn in New York. I felt the stir of loss but tried to deny that distance could change us. I was determined to visit both as I would have my sister, and for a while I did. And then one visit Ellen told me she was pregnant. It became clear she had already told people like her boss, which made me feel way out of her immediate loop. That night she said that she was going to a party if I wanted to come.

"No, I don't want to go to a party." *Don't you realize I flew across the country just to visit you?"*

"You can stay here, then. I won't be long."

That was not what I wanted her to say. I wanted what Deane had said when she pulled up late at the airport, "I didn't want to miss a single minute."

Ellen stayed home. But we were both angry. "You suffocate me," she said.

What I heard was *you are not my sister and I am not yours.* I went in my room and cried until my eyes were swollen. How off the mark I was in my search; I thought I was healing, but I was still looking for Deane everywhere. And Ellen, conscious of it or not, surely felt the burden of my dead sister on her back. How unfair I had been to us both.

The next day, I made an excuse to be out of their house, visiting an old friend. That night Ellen had editors whom I'd worked with over for dinner. I was a distant actress. The next morning I left at 6 a.m. to catch a plane while Ellen and her husband slept.

Our friendship has never recovered, although I know we both care about each other, and we stay in touch. But I understand: I wouldn't want to be anyone's dead sister either.

I grew, as I had with babies, to expect nothing of new friendships, to expect that I wouldn't have them—or certainly not fully satisfying ones. Lynn and I stayed close, but she was far away. And I was close with very old friends who once were friends with both Deane and me, who mourned her as well. But I doubted my singleton self, this new person I was with the wobbly legs and wet back who didn't know how to keep friends without Deane's help. After all, I wasn't sure anymore of my own relationship with myself. And who were these loners who emerged into the world without another human following them? They knew how to be apart and alone. They knew how to make a friend who didn't have to become their identical twin. How did they do that? I knew, even if I didn't want to, I would always look for Deane everywhere.

A few years later, I met a quiet, intuitive woman named Lisa. Like Ellen, she asked me to lunch—and after a while I realized that I had been doing most of the talking. I started laughing,

"You're so good at bringing me out," I said.

I started asking her questions, but pretty soon I was talking again.

Lisa has a knack: if she likes you, she ekes out your shine. You are part of her garden, no flower better than another.

She is, in short, extraordinary, easy to fall into friendship with—as if she knows just where attachment lies and so steps into it—the right slipper this time. When, early in our friendship, I told her about losing Deane, she looked at me with her blue eyes and said, "And she meant everything to you." She wasn't asking a question.

She just got it. Lisa would always have room for Deane in our friendship. She wouldn't be Deane; she didn't have to be. We wouldn't have to talk about it, but Lisa wasn't going to give me any bruises.

We rarely talk about Deane. Sometimes she asks me what grief is like, if it's always there.

"It is when I think too hard. It's easy to go there."

I don't confuse Lisa with Deane. But I learn from her: she has a way of letting her family and friends know she recognizes each of them. One summer the two of us were at a street fair, and she bought us each a beaded bracelet. "Best friend bracelets," she said, laughing, as if we were both fourth graders. I loved it—and I keep the bracelet where I can see it.

She too is now far away in California, but whenever we talk or when I see her she makes me feel valuable. I am the friend she wants. And she is mine.

The notes stop coming. For a long time no one mentions Deane. I stop crying in the shower. It becomes easier to mention her in conversation, to retell family stories for friends without editing Deane out. I even believe I have done the work I need to do to begin a life without her.

So, it takes years to realize I am never without her or the thread of loss that trails behind me. David Grossman, the Israeli writer whose twenty-year-old son was killed in the 2006 war with Lebanon, talks about the struggle to remain himself after his son died. "One has to work very hard . . . to believe in having a future, in wanting to have children. . . . It's an act of choosing life.

"Just imagine," he says, "when most of your being is immersed . . . under the water of death, when the gravity of grief is so strong, really, it's . . . a power that I cannot even describe . . . and yet you manage to uproot . . . yourself, to surface, and not only that but to give life to another human . . . being. It's really heroism."

I thought I was fine. And then I knew I wasn't. The first draft of this book—started eighteen years after Deane's death—was suggested to me many times before I could even consider it. I felt for almost two decades that writing about Deane would make her death my work, and then I would die too. But when an agent suggested thirteen years ago that I write the book, I felt it was time—or thought it was. And still, I realize now how little I was ready to look at what really happened, to focus on Deane and no Deane. So, in the first draft, I had nothing of the actual murder, no facts about Palmer, about his stalk through the office. I, who have researched health articles for decades, would pick up the phone to call the Chelmsford Police Department and begin to gag. I let another year go by and let the phone ring until an officer answered. I explained who I was, who Deane was, asking for the case files.

"Oh, we don't have them," says the officer. "It's too long ago."

In journalism, *No* is never *no*. You go another route. But I was so relieved by this *no*. I hung up and let my heart return to its place.

A year or two later, I call again. It is easier this time—I have the objectivity to ask for the press office. This time I get an officer who listens, who tells me he'll check and send me whatever he finds. A week or so later, a box of materials arrive—the depth of a fat telephone book—a copy of the case file: the police reports, the false sightings, the depositions by each witness. I decide I will look only page by page, in the same order the sheets arrive.

One writing morning, I turn a page, and a police photo appears of Alan Shields's body, the darkened pool around his head. I realize as my stomach squeezes that somewhere in the pile is the moment I must see and cannot see—Deane lying on her office floor. All summer the papers seem to throb, the ventriloquism of my fear. Each morning I read, knowing I would read until the pile was gone, sickened into the summer. If Deane could face this death, then I could too. If she could die this way, I can be there with her. On those days, I weep again in the shower.

One day I called Chelmsford information, asking for Palmer. *The number is unlisted.* I was so glad. I thought, *Well, no wonder.* I was glad for Palmer's mother, his wife, his child. *Good. Stay hidden.*

I tried to find Dr. Shields's wife, learned only that she had remarried, but no one knew her name or where she lived. I found the doctor who attended Deane, but when I left my name and reason for calling, asking him to call me back, he did not. I imagined that he, by now an old man, didn't want to talk about what must have been horrible for him, and I let him be. Because dead ends were a relief. In these journalistic failures, I was lightened, as no true journalist would be. I knew I should go there, to Chelmsford, find the Palmers, find Shields's wife. I couldn't do it.

Nor in the first ten years of writing this book did I talk to my father or my brother of their memories of that day. On its anniversary, we stayed separate, not even calling one another, no ritual to pass between us. I always dwelled on the day of shooting, my father on the day of Deane's actual death. He sometimes told me of dreams about Deane, and his voice would crack, and then so would mine. That was as far as we got.

It's only recently that my brother—at my questioning—has told me details I had no idea of: my shattered face when he arrived; the police visit to the hotel to give my father the autopsy results; my father's focus on finding the best surgeon in the country, his focus only on things he could control.

As Grossman says, grief is a new country, and family may not even travel the same roads or land in the same counties. My brother and I don't talk or see each other often. What bonds us is that we are the only two remaining who know our story, Deane's story.

Have I faced Deane's death? When my father died in 2009, I stepped again into my therapist's office. And what did he find but my sister's death in my arms? In my dreams now, Deane never speaks to me, never talks to me. She is cold, mean—not at all the sister I remember. She is—as my therapist points out gently—dead. After all these years.

I have now moved to a new city and left Deane in the old one.

Who I am without her, I will keep figuring out. But I'm no longer afraid that our separation killed her—or that it will kill me. She was supposed to have another life, and so was I. We won't have that. But maybe if I am lucky, I will finally be able to tell us apart, to believe that Deane's death wasn't ours. When Deane died is not when *we* died. Deane would like that.

Epilogue

Deane stands at my door. I push the screen open, and there she is, her hair the same fiery curls, her smile bright. I lead her into my kitchen, seat her at the table while I put on water to boil. I set cookies on a plate and make mugs of tea, and we move to the sofa. We talk and laugh, but we talk about nothing, about what she's brought, about her plane ride. She slides her suitcase over and pulls out new clothes to show me. Later, Danny comes home, we pour glasses of wine and move to the front porch.

Deane walks in, and nothing I've learned or done or reframed in thirty-one years clouds what I feel.

In these dreams, Deane hasn't aged. She has the same soft face, the same bright hair. I try to give her my new face, but that face doesn't belong to her. I try to imagine my face as her face, but on her it looks wrong. We are no longer identical, the twins to mix up.

For a long time after Deane died, the mirror was a hazardous place. Because there she was. But soon Deane's face disappeared from the mirror, from my memory—as her voice did, as did the small details that distinguish even twins. Slowly in the mirror another person appeared who was not quite Dorothy either. My face had begun its slant toward the center of the earth, no stopping the tug. So, is Deane in the glass now? It's hard to tease apart what genes put there, what loss put there.

This greeting at the door is an indulgence. In fact, I've only felt safe to see this reunion in the last few years. The first time I placed Deane at my door, I didn't know how easily I could draw her inside, how easily we could spill our secrets. But I've not let her come yet from death. She comes to me as if she's been alive all this time, from a life north of here with a husband and children. I do not go too far with this. It is like piecing my way from solid ice to thin slivers. If I indulge in Deane—work to hear her, to see her, to undo all this truth—I will break ice. Nothing good can happen. So I back up. And then I face the other way.

To root in grief feels easy, to lie down and put my face next to Deane's day by day, to think about what she has missed. I understand what it means to pull that face close and feel the air shiver. To grieve as lovers do, as spouses do, as parents do, to realize for the first time that we live on a planet that hangs untethered. And part of the hovering is sweet, where life has gone. If I stay where Deane is most vivid, I sit in the eye of grief where I have not lost or deserted her, betrayed her.

But I don't want to close the shutters on my house. Nor can I. How long can I hold my face there, at the spot where the earth ends? I step back, remember what life is, glad the bullet didn't find me too.

Mine is not the life I expected. I have become a single, relearning intimacy and distance. Deane made friendships count less. On our visits, we sat up in our robes, cross-legged in bed. We talked about the things that scared us, about who we wanted to be, about who we were. We were each other's histories and the story of our happy futures. Hers was the perfect friendship, and anyone who was ever friends with us knew that. Now, without her, friendships are crucial, but for a long time I knew only how to be distant (you are less important than Deane) or intimate (you are Deane). After the funeral, one of Deane's friends took me aside.

"Deane treated her friends like sisters," she told me.

Many of her friends wrote to me for a long time after her death, out of kindness but also searching for the Deane in me, the possibility of the sisterly friendship she was so good at.

"Every Christmas a bag of Snickers would show up in my mailbox from Deane," one friend told me.

For a while I answer their letters, although I never send Snickers. I try becoming friends with Deane's best friend, a hurtful project for both of us. We are all mourning sisterly love.

New friendships have been risky, slow to bloom. But I know better now what to look for. A new friend will not be my sister. But she doesn't have to be.

That life has other entryways is my fortune. Because to summon Deane feels dangerous—like too many drinks. I'm not sure where it might take me, but I am afraid of what I will see when I peer over too often. So I persuade myself that Deane is simply with me the way breath is or the inside of my pocket. And then I turn thoughtless, as I am thoughtless about my own death or about old age. These things lie out there, but I will think about them later.

When someone dies, the world takes its bite. It handles death by changing language, names. Bank accounts dissolve, school records close, car titles transfer, cats get boxed. The world is anxious to sweep up, to present death in formal terms and ask you to sign for it.

Her death took my life too. Except I got a new one with new beliefs, new boundaries, new reverence. Because Deane is dead I no longer think death is the worst that can happen. And I believe in human ignorance about death and what the crows carry to us on their backs. Love cannot be divided like a country. So Deane is with me. She is in my pocket. She is on the airwaves. She filters a mauve sky.

I cannot return to my childhood and talk to the girl I was or the sister I had. But I see those girls in the film that sometimes plays of my life. I know they existed, but I can't touch them.

In this life, I decide who I am: a twin refugee with long skirts and thin sweaters in my cold country. I live as someone else. I have a new life, a new language. I know how to live here on my own.

Sometimes I meet twins. Do I say I am a twin too—or that I was a twin? I decide to let them be. Do not startle these twins with possibilities. Do not let them ask questions they don't want the answers to.

For many years I've wondered what Deane would advise me about living instead of dying. She would ask that I no longer look behind me for her shadow. She would ask me to outlast grief, to wade along to something beyond it. I have. But I am still a twin, with or without her.

Acknowledgments

I began this book thirteen years ago, eighteen after my sister died. I had decided then not to make my life about my sister's death. But when Arielle Eckstut suggested I write about the world of twins and loss, it felt like the time to begin. Along the way, plenty of people have helped me. Anne Krueger, then at Whittle Communications, was the first to ask me to write about losing my sister, and Barbara Paulsen and Nan Wiener, then editors at *Health* magazine agreed to publish an early draft of chapter one: all three gave me the confidence to keep going. I am grateful to the Lowell Police Department for sending me records about the murders at Stoney Brook Counseling Center. I thank Deane's friend and colleague Barbara Kaplan for what must have been a painful phone interview about the worst day in both our lives.

I am grateful to Marian Young for her belief in the book and her efforts to get it published. John Paine is such a good editor—a sharp eye, a gift for language, and an easy way with writers—that I feel motivated to write more books if only to continue working with him. I owe many thanks to my agent Joelle Delbourgo whose realism kept me both grounded and hopeful, and to Perseus/Argo for making publishing with them a classy venture.

I also have to send my love and appreciation to dear friends who read the manuscript in many incarnations: Abigail Esman, whose praise feels exquisite because so is her prose, Alice Daniel, who understands the word *soulmate* better than anyone I know; Elise Nakhnikian, whose close reading, savvy suggestions, and praise almost match her wonderful ability at friendship; and Laura Kaster, who read the book in one sitting, and who understands as well as anyone what her dear friend Deane meant to both of us.

I thank my sons, Jacob and Matthew, for sending their wonderful lives my way. I thank my brother, Jeff, for understanding and honoring, often better than I do, all that connects us. And most of all, I thank the forbearing Dan Foltz-Gray for reading this book at almost every stage, for believing it would be published, and for keeping me laughing. It's he who handed me a mended heart.

Author's Note

Most of the events in this book are now decades old. I describe the events to the best of my recollection. I have changed many names to protect people's privacy.

About the Author

Dorothy Foltz-Gray has been a freelance writer and editor specializing in health, fitness, food, and personal essays for eighteen years. A former editor of books (business and medical) and magazines (fiction, lifestyle) at Whittle Communications in Knoxville, Tennessee, she is the author of *Clean Sweep: The Principles of an American Entrepreneur and the Company He Founded; Make Pain Disappear; Alternative Treatments for Arthritis: An A to Z Guide;* and co-author of *Food Cures.* Her work has appeared in *Bon Appetit; Cooking Light; Good Housekeeping; Health; Ladies Home Journal; Parenting; Prevention; O, The Oprah Magazine; Reader's Digest; Redbook; Real Simple; Woman's Day;* and others. She is a winner of the Tennessee Arts Commission Fellowship for Poetry; a Mature Media Gold Award; and an East Tennessee Society of Professional Journalists Award of Excellence. She lives in Asheville, North Carolina, with her husband, Dan.

CPSIA information can be obtained at www.ICGtesting.com
Printed in the USA
LVOW07s0535300816

502396LV00003BA/237/P